THE PROPHETS
IN *BARZAKH*
and
THE HADITH OF
ISRÂ' AND *MI'RÂJ*
by

AL-SAYYID MUHAMMAD
IBN 'ALAWI

followed by

THE IMMENSE
MERITS OF *AL-SHÂM*
and
THE VISION OF ALLAH ﷻ

2nd edition

Translation and Notes by
Gibril Fouad Haddad
Damascus
1420/1999

This work is humbly dedicated to

Sultan al-Awliya' Mu'ayyid al-Din wa al-Sunna Mawlana al-Shaykh Muhammad Nazim Adil al-Qubrusi al-Naqshbandi al-Haqqani,

to his Deputy

Shaykh Muhammad Hisham Kabbani

and to

Al-Shaykh al-Sayyid Muhammad ibn al-Sayyid 'Alawi al-Maliki al-Hasani
and to their friends and followers worldwide.

《Lo! my Protecting Friend is Allah who revealed the Book. He befriends the righteous.》
(7:196)

ISBN: 95-930409-00-1

Published by:
As-Sunna Foundation of America
2415 Owen Rd Ste B
Fenton, MI 48430
email: asfa@sunnah.org

www.sunnah.org
www.islamicsupremecouncil.org

Foreword

Bismillahir-Rahmanir-Raheem

All praise is due to Allah Almighty who has revived in the hearts of His servants thirst for understanding the Islamic doctrine, *al-'aqeedah.* Blessings and salutations on His Beloved Servant Muhammad 襄, whom He raised to the station of nearness and whom he blessed with the revelation of Divine Guidance.

As-Sunna Foundation of America is honored to make available to the reading public this new set of translations of classical Islamic texts – the *Islamic Doctrines and Beliefs* series. We congratulate Dr. Gabriel Haddad for his efforts in bringing these outstanding classical manuscripts to light in the English language, as these books are a necessity for every Muslim home, school, library and university.

These works have reached us through distant centuries, authored by scholars who spent the whole of their lives in devotion to Allah and to spreading the knowledge of His great religion. They will undoubtedly stand witness for their authors on the Day of Judgment, wherein *"Whoever works righteousness benefits his own soul"* [41: 46], for every drop of blood running in the veins of such pious and sincere sages was infused with their intense devotion to preserve the fundamentals and the branches of Islam. Reliance on classical texts such as these leaves little room for the introduction of alien creeds or uneducated speculation. Due to the extravagant efforts scholars made to compile these books, they are comprehensible and applicable to the general reader and student of religion.

Likewise the efforts of Dr. Haddad, who spent long days and nights in perfecting these translations, is something that we pray will be highly rewarded in this life and the next, for his intention and ours is to broadcast and clarify the pure and unadulterated teachings of *Ahl as-Sunna wal-Jama'a,* The People of the Sunnah and the Majority, whose foundations were laid by the Prophet 襄 under the direction of his Lord, whose walls were erected by the *Salaf as-saliheen,* the pious predecessors, and whose roof and domes were built by the *Khalaf as-sadiqeen,* the truthful successors up to the present age.

The Importance of Knowledge of Correct 'Aqeedah

Due to the fact that every generation witnesses a silent decline in worshippers' knowledge of the fundamental doctrines and beliefs of religion, constant efforts are required to elucidate and preserve the sources of this knowledge and to preserve them in the hearts and minds of Allah's servants. The acquisition of knowledge is obligatory for every accountable Muslim, for without it the appearance of conjecture and uneducated opinion is inevitable. Therein lies a danger that leads to an erroneous understanding of faith, which if left unchecked, may lead the seeker to a dangerous precipice from which he is unable to escape a serious fall.

The correct understanding of the signs of Allah Almighty, His Angels, His Books, His Prophets, the Day of Judgment, and the Divine Decree saves one from two extremes: denial of Allah's attributes, and its opposite anthropomorphism, the relating of Allah's attributes to physical manifestations.

There is no time better than today to introduce these books to those for whom English is the mother tongue, for the subject of 'aqeedah has become one of controversy and confusion. These books provide a classical approach to understanding Islamic doctrine, based on some of the most accepted and reliable scholars of *Ahl as-Sunnah wal-Jama'ah*, the Saved Group.

The Honored Status of Muhammad ﷺ

Today a growing number of Muslims are seeking a real understanding of the noble status of Muhammad ﷺ after he departed from this world to the Divine Presence. This work by As-Sayyid Muhammad Ibn 'Alawi on this topic has been translated for the first time, assisting the believer in putting aside doubts concerning the reality of the life of the prophets in the *barzakh,* the other-worldly isthmus between this life and the heavenly one.

Ibn 'Alawi provides a comprehensive and authentic account of the Night Journey and Ascension, *al-isra wal-mi'raj,* in which Allah honored *al-*

Buraq to carry the Best of Creation ﷺ from Makkah to the Farthest Mosque in Jerusalem, and from there to ascend into the highest Heavens. Therein the Prophet ﷺ was shown the wonders of Paradise and the perils of Hell, and of what is to come. The climax of this ultimate journey was the Prophet's ﷺ meeting his Lord. There and then no one knows what took place at the station of *"two bow's length or closer,"* a station in which some scholars affirm the Prophet ﷺ was granted the vision of his Lord.

Praise be to Allah, Lord of the Worlds, and salutations and blessings of peace on His Perfect Servant, Muhammad ﷺ.

Shaykh Muhammad Hisham Kabbani
1 Ramadan, 1420
December 8, 1999
Fenton, Michigan, USA

Contents

About al-Sayyid Muhammad ibn 'Alawi

Al-Shaykh al-Sayyid Dr. Muhammad ibn al-Sayyid 'Alawi ibn al-Sayyid 'Abbas ibn al-Sayyid 'Abd al-'Aziz al-Maliki al-Hasani al-Makki al-Ash'ari al-Shadhili is the educator of *Ahl al-Sunna* and light of the Prophet's House 鑾 in our time, a major contemporary scholar of hadith, commentary of Qur'an, Law, doctrine, *tasawwuf*, and Prophetic biography *(sîra)*, he is presently the most highly respected authority of *Ahl al-Sunna* in the Mother of Cities. Both his father (d. 1971CE) and grandfather were the imams and head preachers of the Sacred Mosque in Mecca, as was Sayyid Muhammad himself beginning in 1971 and until 1983, at which time he was barred from office after the publication of his book *Mafahim Yajib an Tusahhah*.

Sayyid Muhammad was educated from childhood by his father in the sources of Islam as well as by other noted Meccan scholars such as Sayyid Amin Kutbi, Hassan Masshat, Muhammad Nur Sayf, Sa'id Yamani, and others. He received his Ph.D. in Hadith Studies with the highest merits from al-Azhar of Egypt at the age of twenty-five. He then travelled in the pursuit of hadith studies to North Africa, the Middle East, Turkey, Yemen, and the Indo-Pakistani Subcontinent, obtaining teaching certificates *(ijâzât)* and chains of transmission from Imam Habib Ahmad Mashhur al-Haddad, Shaykh Hasanayn Makhluf, the Ghumari brothers of Morocco, Shaykh Dya' al-Din Qadiri of Madina, Mawlana Zakariyya Kandihlawi, and numerous others.

The Shaykh has authored more than a hundred books, treatises, and articles in Arabic on various topics in the Islamic sciences. Among his most famous works:

- *Abwab al-Faraj* ("The Gates of Deliverance"),[1] a descriptive manual of supplications and devotions for various occasions from the Qur'an, the Sunna, and the Imams of Islam together with a description of the manners of supplicants. It contains a valuable prescription for reciting the *Fatiha* frequently.

- *Al-Anwar al-Bahiyya min Isra' wa Mi'raj Khayr al-Bariyya* ("The Resplendent Lights of the Night Journey and Ascension of the Best of Creation"),[2] a monograph that collates all the sound narrations of the Prophet's 𐭀 night journey and ascension into a single narrative, translated in full in the present book.[3]

- *Al-Bayan wa al-Ta'rif fi Dhikra al-Mawlid al-Sharif* ("The Exposition and Definition of the Celebration of the Noble Birthday"),[4] a concise anthology of texts and poems related to the subject.

- *Hawl al-Ihtifal bi Dhikra al-Mawlid al-Nabawi al-Sharif* ("Regarding the Celebration of the Prophet's 𐭀 Birthday"),[5] a meticulous summation of the proofs adduced by the scholars for the permissibility of celebrating the *mawlid*.[6]

- *Al-Husun al-Mani'a* ("The Invincible Forts"), a booklet of personal devotions selected from the Sunna and the practice of the *Salaf*.

---

[1] Cairo: Dar al-Ja'fari, n.d.
[2] Second ed. Riyadh: n. p., 1998.
[3] A full English translation was first published in Shaykh Hisham Kabbani's *Encyclopedia of Islamic Doctrine*.
[4] Published by the author, 1995.
[5] Tenth edition, Cairo: Dar Jawami' al-Kalim, 1998. Most of its material was incorporated into Shaykh Hisham Kabbani's section on the *mawlid* in his *Encyclopedia*.
[6] On this topic see also 'Izz al-Din Husayn al-Shaykh, al-Adilla al-Shar'iyya fi Jawaz al-Ihtifal bi Milad Khayr al-Bariyya (1993).

- *Huwa Allah* ("⟨He is Allah⟩"), a statement of Sunni doctrine in refutation of the aberrations of anthropomorphism.

- *Khulasa Shawariq al-Anwar min Ad'iya al-Sada al-Akhyar* ("The Epitome of the Rising Lights Taken From the Supplications of the Elect Masters"), a manual of devotions taken from the Sunna and the Imams of Islam. It contains, among other precious supplications, the devotion *(hizb)* of Imam al-Nawawi which begins with the words:

  > In the name of Allah, Allah is greatest! I say upon myself, my Religion, my spouses, my children, my property, my friends, their Religion and their property, a thousandfold "There is no change nor power except with Allah the Exalted, the Almighty."

- *Al-Madh al-Nabawi Bayn al-Ghuluw wa al-Insaf* ("The Panegyric of the Prophet ﷺ Between Extremism and Fairness"),[7] a study of the genre with examples from the Qur'an, hadith, commentaries, and poetry showing that praising the Prophet ﷺ is part of the perfection of one's Islam and not, as some enviers have claimed, a contravention of the hadith: "Do not over-extol me *(la tutruni)* the way Christians over-extolled 'Isa ibn Maryam [i.e. by divinizing him]."[8]

- *Mafahim Yajib an Tusahhah* ("The Necessary Corrections of Certain Misconceptions"),[9] perhaps the most important contemporary statement of *Ahl al-Sunna* on "Salafi" teachings. In this book Shaykh Muhammad ibn 'Alawi establishes the proofs and positions of the Imams of *Ahl al-Sunna* on the topics of *tasawwuf, tawassul*, the Prophet's ﷺ intercession, the celebration of his birthday or *mawlid*, the

---

[7]Cairo: Dar Wahdan, n.d.
[8]Narrated from 'Umar by al-Bukhari, Ahmad, Malik, and al-Darimi.
[9]Tenth ed. Madina, 1999.

Ash'ari school, etc. with extensive documentation including the sources claimed as authoritative by the "Salafis" themselves.

• *Mafhum al-Tatawwur wa al-Tajdid fi al-Shari'a al-Islamiyya* ("What is Meant By Growth And Renewal In Islamic Law"),

• *Manhaj al-Salaf fi Fahm al-Nusus Bayn al-Nazariyya wa al-Tatbiq* ("The Methodology of the Predecessors in Understanding the Texts: Theory and Practice"), his latest work, a continuation and update of the *Mafahim* from which we translated the section entitled "The Prophets in *Barzakh*" in the present book.

• *Muhammad* 🌼 *al-Insan al-Kamil* ("Muhammad 🌼 the Perfect Human Being"),[10] a comprehensive summary of the Prophet's 🌼 attributes in the manner of the books of *shamâ'il*.[11] Its chapters are titled as follows:

"The Perfection of His Lofty Gifts and Pure Attributes."

"The Perfection of His Immunity From Defects and Questionable Aspects, and Allah's Safeguarding Him From Enemies, Devils, and Offences."

"The Perfection of His Magnificent Manners and Noble Qualities."

---

[10]Fourth ed. Madina: Matabi' al-Rashid, 1990.
[11]E.g. al-Tirmidhi, *al-Shama'il*; al-Qadi 'Iyad, *al-Shifa'*; al-Baghawi, *al-Anwar fi Shama'il al-Nabi al-Mukhtar*; Abu Nu'aym, al-Bayhaqi, and others: *Dala'il al-Nubuwwa*, al-Qastallani, *al-Mawahib al-Ladu-niyya* and its commentary by al-Zurqani; al-Suyuti, *al-Khasa'is al-Kubra* and *al-Riyad al-Aniqa*; Shams al-Din Muhammad ibn Yusuf al-Shami al-Salihi, *Subul al-Huda wa al-Rashad fi Sira Khayr al-'Ibad* compiled from over three hundred sources; al-Nabahani, *Shawahid al-Haqq*; Shaykh 'Abd Allah Siraj al-Din, *Sayyiduna Muhammad* 🌼 etc.

"The Perfection of His Illustrious Merits and Peerless Traits."

"The Perfection of His Wisdom in Government and Military Leadership."

"The Perfection of His Conduct in the Administration and Education of the Community, and His Heedful Interaction With Them in General, and with His Family and Companions in Particular."

"The Perfection of His Law and Its Fulfillment of Human Needs and Keeping Pace With the Spirit of the Times Without Incurring Alteration Nor Substitution."

- *Al-Mustashriqun Bayn al-Insaf wa al-'Asabiyya* ("The Orientalists Between Fairness and Prejudice"),[12] a brief survey of the pitfalls of literature on Islam by non-Muslims.

- *Al-Qawa'id al-Asasiyya fi 'Ulum al-Qur'an* ("Basic Foundations in the Sciences of the Qur'an"),[13] a useful primer and introduction to Dr. Nur al-Din 'Itr's *'Ulum al-Qur'an al-Karim* ("The Sciences of the Noble Qur'an").[14]

- *Al-Qawa'id al-Asasiyya fi Usul al-Fiqh* ("Basic Foundations in the Principles of the Law"),[15] a useful primer and introduction to Dr. Wahba al-Zuhayli's two-volume *Usul al-Fiqh al-Islami.*[16]

- *Al-Qudwa al-Hasana fi Manhaj al-Da'wa ila Allah* ("The Excellent Examplar in the Method of Calling Others Unto Allah").[17]

---

[12]Jeddah: Matabi' Sahar, 1982.
[13]Mecca: Published by the author, 1999.
[14]Sixth ed. Damascus: Matba'a al-Sabah, 1996.
[15]Mecca: Published by the author, 1999.
[16]Damascus: Dar al-Fikr, 1986.
[17]Tenth ed. Madina, 1999.

- *Qul Hadhihi Sabili* ("❨Say: This Is My Way❩ (12:108)"), a concise manual of Islamic doctrine and morals.

- *Al-Risala al-Islamiyya Kamaluha wa Khuluduha wa 'Alamiyyatuha* ("The Message of Islam: Its Perfection, Immortality, and Universality").[18]

- *Shifa' Al-Fu'ad bi Ziyara Khayr Al-'Ibad* ("The Healing of Hearts Concerning the Visitation of the Best of Human Beings"), which establishes the proofs and positions of the Imams of *Ahl al-Sunna* on the subject of traveling to visit the Prophet 鐖 in order to obtain blessings *(tabarrukan)* and intercession *(tashaffu'an)*.

- *Al-Tali' al-Sa'id al-Muntakhab Min al-Musalsalat wa al-Asanid* ("The New Moon of Happiness: A Selection of Similarly-Narrated Hadiths and Chains").[19]

- *Tarikh al-Hawadith wa al-Ahwal al-Nabawiyya* ("Historical Events and Markers in the Prophet's 鐖 Life").[20]

- *Al-'Uqud al-Lu'lu'iyya bi al-Asanid al-'Alawiyya* ("The Pearl Necklaces: 'Alawi's Transmission Chains"),[21] in which the Shaykh lists the transmission chains he received from his father, al-Sayyid 'Alawi ibn 'Abbas al-Maliki.

- *Wa Huwa bi al-Ufuq al-A'la* ("❨When He was on the uppermost horizon❩ (53:7)"),[22] the most comprehensive commentary to date on the Prophet's 鐖 night journey and ascension, summing up over forty works devoted to the subject. A companion to the Shaykh's *al-Anwar al-Bahiyya*, the book contains a detailed commentary of the verses that

---

[18]Ed. Najih Maymun al-Indonisi. Jeddah: Matabi' Sahar, 1990.
[19]Second ed. Mecca: Matabi' al-Safa, 1992.
[20]Twelfth ed. Jeddah: Matabi' Sahar, 1996.
[21]Second ed.
[22]Cairo: Dar Jawami' al-Kalim, 1999.

pertain to the vision of Allah ﷻ and a full documentation of the authentic relevant narrations.

Sayyid Muhammad ibn 'Alawi is dearly loved by the people of Mecca, Madina, and the Hijaz. Since his forced retirement from public teaching and preaching, he has devoted himself to the private education of hundreds of students in Islamic studies, with emphasis on South-East Asian nationals, at his residence and mosque on al-Maliki street in the Rusayfa district of Mecca. Dr. Zuhayr Kutbi of Mecca wrote his biography which was published in Egypt in 1995.[23]

---

[23]Notes graciously provided by Shaykh Fakhroddin Owaisi al-Madani, may Allah reward him for it.

I.
The Prophets in *Barzakh*[24]

"The proofs and the transmitted texts have been established
as authentic in the highest degree that the Prophet ﷺ is alive
and tender... that he fasts and performs pilgrimage every year,
and that he purifies himself with water which rains on him."
Al-Haytami, *Al-Jawhar al-Munazzam*.

"The work of the next world is all *dhikr* and *du'â'*"
Al-Nawawi, *Sharh Sahih Muslim*.

"It is obligatory knowledge to know that the Prophet's ﷺ body is,
in the earth, tender and humid [as in life], and when the Companions
asked him: "How is our greeting presented to you after you have turned
to dust?" he replied: "Allah has defended the earth from consuming the
flesh of Prophets," and if his body were not in his grave
he would not have given this answer."
Ibn al-Qayyim, *al-Ruh*.

I.   Allah's ﷺ Saying ❨Verily You Shall Die❩ (39:30)

We often hear certain people repeat the above verse of
Qur'an and other verses of similar import as proofs for denying
the human perfections and Prophetic characteristics whereby our
master Muhammad ﷺ is distinguished from the remainder of
human beings. Among those verses is Allah's saying: ❨**We
appointed immortality for no mortal before you. What! if
you die, can they be immortal?**❩ (21:34).

---

[24]From Shaykh Muhammad ibn 'Alawi's book *Manhaj al-Salaf* (p.
182-207).

Now, who denies those explicit verses? Who claims that the Prophet ﷺ is still alive exactly in the same way as he was alive in the world? Surely, no one makes such claims except a dull-witted, ignorant person who has not the least acquaintance with the Qur'an and Sunna. But he who cites these verses has overlooked – either by design or ignorance – to warn people that such verses have come to show that our master Muhammad ﷺ is subject to the same death to which all human beings are subject, and that it is Allah ﷻ alone Who is the Eternally Remaining, the Living Who Does Not Die.

The fact seems hidden from the minds of these would-be objectors that the noble verses which declare this important truth – whereby the Prophet ﷺ is a human being and that he shall die just as human beings die – were only revealed for a specific reason: to correct a widespread misconception and aberration that prevailed in the mindsets of the Time of Ignorance. This aberration consisted in linking together, on the one hand, human perfections and merits by which a man was known, and, on the other hand, life. They believed that when a man died, his merit ended and so did his perfection, as well as anything for which he was held to be special. By dying, he was losing all value and all merit, and his values and qualities died with him. Accordingly, those verses came to show the falsehood and complete invalidity of this position.

The verses came to tell Abu Jahl, Abu Lahab, the masses of idol-worshippers, and all those who are cut from the same cloth, that our master Muhammad ﷺ is a human being and that he is not an immortal walking on the face of the earth. Rather, he will be subject to whatever human beings undergo in their totality – but that does not diminish his perfections nor affect his rank nor lower his level. For he is a human being, not an immortal, and the day of his death shall come – as death is forewritten for every human being as Allah ﷻ has said: ⟪Every

soul shall taste death (3:185). However, such death never changes his high station and merit! It is as if He were saying to them: "Beware lest one of you think of the Prophet's ﷺ station in disparaging terms at the time he dies, and imagine, at that time, that he no longer benefits nor serves a purpose nor hears nor replies nor supplicates nor intercedes!"

These verses came to show these truths explicitly. People were in denial of Resurrection and Judgment. Their spokesmen would say: "It is nothing more than wombs that thrust and earth that swallows; nothing but Time causes us to die."[25] The Qur'an is replete with verses that show us such positions of theirs, which entail the denial of the isthmus-life *(al-hayât al-barzakhiyya)* between death and Resurrection and the attending Paradise-life or torture of the grave, as in His sayings:

{They shall surely say: "There is nothing but our first death, and we shall not be raised again. Bring back our fathers, if you speak the truth!" Are they better, or the folk of Tubba and those before them? We destroyed them, for surely they were guilty. And We created not the heavens and the earth, and all that is between them, in play. We created them not save with truth; but most of them know not. Assuredly the Day of Decision is the term of all of them.} (44:34-40).

{And man says: "What! When I am dead, shall I then be brought forth alive?" Does not man remember that We created him before, when he was nothing?} (19:66-67).

---

[25]Ibn al-Qayyim, *Hidaya al-Hayara fi Ajwiba al-Yahud wa al-Nasara* (p. 4).

❨And they say: "There is nothing but our life of the world; we die and we live, and nothing destroys us save Time" when they have no knowledge whatsoever of (all) that; they do but guess. And when Our clear revelations are recited unto them their only argument is that they say: "Bring (back) our fathers then, if you are truthful." Say (unto them, O Muhammad): Allah gives life to you, then causes you to die, then gathers you unto the Day of Resurrection whereof there is no doubt. But most of mankind know not.❩ (45:24-26).

❨And he has coined for Us a similitude, and has forgotten the fact of his creation, saying: Who will revive these bones when they have rotted away? Say: He will revive them Who produced them at the first, for He is Knower of every creation❩ (36:78-79).

That is why the Truthful and Trusting one – al-Siddiq ☙ – announced this truth saying: "Whoever worshipped Muhammad ☙, let him know that Muhammad has died, and whoever worshipped Allah ☙, let him know that He is the Living One Who Never Dies."[26]

At this point some of those whom Allah has forsaken come and cite the verse: ❨Verily you shall die and verily they will die❩ (39:30) together with other Qur'anic texts and Prophetic hadiths of related meaning, attempting to use them as proofs for their own corrupt designs and ill intentions. This is in order to cast aspersions on the perfections of the Prophet Muhammad ☙ and so as to assert for him ordinary humanity as well as equality between the noblest of all Prophetic Messengers and all other human beings.

---

[26]Narrated from 'A'isha and Ibn 'Abbas by al-Bukhari.

How much have we heard and read on the part of one of them who blackened many a page saying that the Prophet ﷺ neither hears nor benefits anyone! Impudence and lack of manners have reached such a point in one of them that he says: "If you were to come to the Prophet's ﷺ grave and ask of him the smallest worldly service such as a dirham or a cup of water, he will be incapable of giving it to you." I ask, what does the dim-witted writer of the above words know of those who seek a means *(wasîla)* in the Prophet ﷺ or ask him something? They are only asking him to ask Allah for them. This is due to the Prophet's ﷺ immense rank and pre-eminence in Allah's presence.

Furthermore, one does not ask for lowly matters which do not come to mind except to those that worship this lowly world and run after money and property – those who will not earn anything more than this worldly race and competition in the accumulation of wealth. The Prophet ﷺ told us about this kind of people when he said: "He has perished and failed!"[27] This is actually an invocation against them that Allah make them perish and fail, as well as a report that this is their actual condition. We seek refuge in Allah!

This is our answer to those who want a scientific examination of the question, without passion, partisanship, or obduracy, and who want to tread the path of the People of Truth

---

[27]Narrated from Abu Hurayra by al-Bukhari and Ibn Majah: "Perish the worshipper of gold and silver and contention, who agrees when he is given and, when he does not get anything, becomes angry. He has perished and failed! [Or: Perish, and failure to him!] If adversity come to him, may it not go away. Blessing and everything good to the servant who holds the reins of his horse in the path of Allah. His hair is disheveled, his feet dusty; on his watch he watches, in the rear guard he stands rear guard; if he asks permission he is not granted it, and if he intercedes he is not granted his request."

– meaning the people of high manners, refinement, and true
knowledge. Upon such it is incumbent to let discourse reflect the
understanding:

- that the Prophet's 襲 perfections endure and remain
  entirely preserved without the slightest doubt;

- that he hears spoken words, replies to the *salâm* given,
  praises Allah for the good deeds of his *Umma* that are
  shown to him, and asks forgiveness for the evil ones;

- that showing excellent manners with him at his *maqâm*
  upon visiting him, greeting him with our *salâm* at his
  grave, in his mosque, and in his *Rawda*, are all among
  the most stringent obligations and the most binding of
  duties;

- that "his sanctity after he died is exactly as his sanctity
  when he was alive," as stated by the Imam of the Abode
  of Emigration to the Abbasid Caliph;[28]

- and that even though he 襲 died and his body has
  undoubtedly disappeared from our sights – for none
  eternally remains except the One Alone, the Living, the

---

[28]Narrated from Malik by al-Qadi 'Iyad in *al-Shifa* (2:92-93) and Ibn
Qunfudh in *Wasila al-Islam* (p. 145-146). Stated, without attribution to
Malik, by al-'Abdari, *al-Taj wa al-Iklil* (3:400), al-Hattab, *Mawahib al-
Jalil* (3:400), al-Bahuti, *Kashshaf al-Qanna'* (2:516-517), and al-
Shirwani, *Hawashi Tuhfa al-Muhtaj* (2:164). 'Iyad's chain was graded
as "weak or forged" *(sic)* by Sulayman ibn 'Abd Allah ibn Muhammad
ibn 'Abd al-Wahhab in his book *Taysir al-'Aziz al-Hamid fi Sharh
Kitab al-Tawhid* (p. 312), following in this Ibn Taymiyya and his
student Ibn 'Abd al-Hadi in *al-Sarim al-Munki* (p. 244). However, the
hadith master *Shaykh al-Islam* Ibn Jama'a said in *Hidaya al-Salik*
(3:1381): "The report is related by the two hadith masters Ibn
Bushkuwal and al-Qadi 'Iyad in *al-Shifa'*, and no attention is paid to
the words of those who claim that it is forged purely on the basis of
their idle desires."

Self-Sustaining Who never tires nor sleeps –
nevertheless, he is alive with a complete isthmus-life
(hayât barzakhiyya) which is greater and better and more
perfect than worldly life – indeed, higher, dearer,
sweeter, more perfect, and more beneficial than worldly
life.

It is enough that those who enjoy this isthmus-life are
described as possessing three magnificent attributes related to
perfection: life *(hayât)*, sustenance *(rizq)*, and being-with-Allah
('indiyya). These attributes are expressed in Allah's saying:
❰**They live, finding their sustenance in the presence of their
lord**❱ (3:169). If this was said about the martyrs *(al-shuhadâ')*,
who have a lesser rank than the Prophets, than what about the
latter? Allah's blessings and peace upon them!

II. The Isthmus-Life of Prophets: Proof-Texts

The proof-texts for the life of Prophets in the grave are
numerous. We shall mention some of them. They provide
healing, Allah willing, for anyone in whose heart there is
sickness.

  1. The Prophet ﷺ said: "The Prophets are alive in their
     graves, praying." *(Al-anbiyâ'u ahyâ'un fî qubûrihim
     yusallûn.)* [29]

---

[29]Narrated from Anas by Abu Ya'la in his *Musnad* (6:147) with a
sound chain as stated by al-Haythami in *Majma' al-Zawa'id* (8:211) –
confirmed by Abu Ya'la's editor Shaykh Husayn Asad – and by al-
Bayhaqi in *Hayat al-Anbiya' fi Quburihim* with a sound chain as stated
by Ibn Hajar in *Fath al-Bari* (1959 ed. 6:487); also by al-Bazzar in his
Musnad with two weak chains as indicated by Ibn Hajar (*ibid.* and
Mukhtasar 2:271-272 #1852-1853) because of al-Hasan ibn Qutayba as
shown by Ibn 'Adi in *al-Kamil* (2:327) and Ibn Hajar in *Lisan al-Mizan*

It is narrated by al-Bayhaqi and Abu Ya'la from Anas and is a sound *(sahîh)* hadith. [See also **#1a** below, following **#5**.] Al-Munawi said:

> This is because they are like martyrs – rather, their lives are higher than that of martyrs, and the latter are ❰**finding their sustenance in the presence of their lord**❱ (3:169). The purpose of specifying their being-with-Allah is to allude to the fact that their life is not visible to us. It is more like the life of the angels. It is likewise with Prophets. That is why the latter are not inherited from, nor can one marry their wives after them.[30]

Al-Bayhaqi said in his book *al-I'tiqad*:

> The Prophets – Allah's blessings and peace upon them – after they die, their souls are returned back to them and so they are alive ❰**in the presence of their lord**❱ like the martyrs. Our Prophet 🕌 saw, on the Night of the Ascension, a number of them.[31] We have compiled a monograph establishing the facts of their life in the grave.[32]

2. Abu Dawud narrated with a sound *(sahîh)* chain – as stated by al-Subki – from Abu Hurayra that Allah's

---

(2:246). It is also narrated by Tamam al-Razi (d. 414) in *al-Fawa'id* (1:33) and al-Suyuti in *Anba' al-Adhkiya' bi Hayat al-Anbiya'* (#5) – reproduced in full in his *al-Hawi li al-Fatawa* – who adds: "The life of the Prophet in his grave and that of the rest of the prophets is known to us as definitive knowledge *('ilman qat'iyyan)*." See also al-Albani, *Silsila Sahiha* (#621).

[30]Al-Munawi, *Fayd al-Qadir* (3:184).
[31]See Part **II**.
[32]Al-Bayhaqi, *al-I'tiqad* (1981 ed. p. 305).

Messenger 鬱 said: "No-one greets me except that Allah has returned my soul to me so that I may greet him back." *(Mâ min ahadin yusallimu 'alayya illâ radd Allâhu 'alayya rûhî hattâ arudda 'alayhi al-salâm.)* [33] [Also see below, #2a.]

Al-Bayhaqi began his chapter on the visit to the Prophet's 鬱 grave with this hadith.[34] A number of the Imams have relied upon this hadith, among them Imam Ahmad. Al-Subki said: "It is correct to rely upon it due to the merit of the Prophet's 鬱 soul, which is immense."

If it is said that his words in this hadith: "Allah has returned my soul to me so that I may greet him back" indicate the impermanency of life, the answer is manyfold:

- Al-Bayhaqi used this hadith as proof for the life of Prophets in the grave. He said: "What is meant – and Allah knows best – is: 'except that Allah has once and for all returned my soul to me so that I may greet him back.'"[35]

- Al-Subki said: "It is possible that it be a spiritual return of the soul and that his noble soul is actually

---

[33]Narrated from Abu Hurayra by Abu Dawud with a chain declared sound by al-Nawawi in *Riyad al-Salihin* and *al-Adhkar*, Ibn al-Qayyim as stated by al-'Azim Abadi in *'Awn al-Ma'bud* (6:22), Ibn Hajar in *Fath al-Bari* (1959 ed. 6:488), al-Wadyashi in *Tuhfa al-Muhtaj* (2:190), al-'Ajluni in *Kashf al-Khafa'* (2:253), and al-Shawkani in *Nayl al-Awtar*. Also narrated from Abu Hurayra with sound chains by Ahmad in his *Musnad* and al-Bayhaqi in *al-Sunan al-Kubra* (5:245 #1040); al-Bayhaqi in *Shu'ab al-Iman* (2:217, 3:490-491); and al-Tabarani in *al-Awsat* (3:262) with a weak chain as indicated by al-Haythami in *Majma' al-Zawa'id* (10:162).

[34]Al-Bayhaqi, *al-Sunan al-Kubra* (5:245), *Bâb Ziyârati Qabr al-Nabi* 鬱.

[35]Al-Bayhaqi, *Shu'ab al-Iman* (3:491).

engaged in the contemplation of the Exalted Presence and the Highest Assembly, away from this world, so that whenever one greets him, his soul comes forth to this world to receive this greeting and returns it. That is, the 'return' of his noble soul is actually a spiritual glance *(iltifât rûhânî)* and condescension *(tanazzul)* to the human realms, away from immersion in the Highest Presence."

• One of the scholars said: "It is a kind of discourse phrased according to the capacity for comprehension of those to whom it is addressed, concerning one who has left this world. Its message is that the soul is necessarily returned so that he may hear and reply. It is as if he had said: 'I answer one's greeting in the fullest sense of the word.' This also indicates that the Prophet's ﷺ soul was returned to im upon the greeting of the first person to greet him [after his death], and that it does not mean that it is seized again after that. Nor did anyone claim that such a phenomenon repeat itself, for it would lead to an unlimited succession of deaths! This said, we believe and assert that all the dead possess perception such as knowledge and hearing, *a fortiori* the Prophets. We categorically declare the reality of life returning to every deceased person in their graves as established in the Sunna. Life returns to them so that they may be questioned. It is obligatory to believe this, as is belief in the delight or torture of the grave, and the perceiving of all these phenomena for which life is a precondition. Someone may say: 'If they were alive we would see them.' We answer: The angels are alive, the martyrs are alive, the jinn are alive, yet we do not see them. Still, it is possible to see them, since everything that exists may be seen. Imam al-Suyuti – may Allah have mercy on him! – wrote a booklet entitled *Nur al-Halak fi Jawaz Ru'ya al-Jinn wa al-Malak* ("The Possibility of Seeing the Jinn and the Angels"),[36] and in it he also addressed the possibility of seeing the Prophet ﷺ. For all this he produced proofs, and may Allah reward him well for it."[37]

3. Another proof is the hadith narrated from Abu al-Darda' whereby the Prophet ﷺ said: "Make abundant invocations of blessings upon me the day of *Jum'a,* for that day is witnessed by the angels. Verily, no-one invokes blessings upon me except his invocation is shown to me until he finishes it." Abu al-Darda' said: "Even after death?" The Prophet ﷺ replied: "Even after death! Verily, Allah has forbidden the earth from consuming the bodies of Prophets. Therefore Allah's Prophet is alive and sustained!" *(Akthirû al-salâta 'alayya yawma al-jumu'a fa innahu mashhûdun tashhaduhu al-malâ'ikatu wa inna ahadan lan yusalliya 'alayya illâ 'uridat 'alayya salâtuhu hattâ yafrughu minhâ. Qâla qultu wa ba'da al-mawt? Qâla wa ba'da al-mawti inna Allâha harrama 'alâ al-ardi an ta'kula ajsâda al-anbiyâ'i fa nabiyyullâhi hayyun yurzaq.)* [38]

---

[36]Reproduced in full in *al-Hawi li al-Fatawa.*
[37]See also al-Haytami, *Fatawa Hadithiyya* (p. 297). It is known that Abu al-'Abbas al-Mursi – Abu al-Hasan al-Shadhili's shaykh – used to say: "If I ceased to see the Prophet ﷺ for one moment, I would no longer count myself a Muslim."
[38]Narrated from Abu al-Darda' by Ibn Majah with a *munqati'* chain missing a sub-narrator in two places. However, its parts are confirmed verbatim by other sound narrations, among them Aws's narration cited below. Consequently the hadith master al-Busiri declared it sound in his *Zawa'id* (2:58-59). The first part (concerning the order to invoke more blessings on *Jum'a* and the disclosure of this invocation to the Prophet) is related by al-Bayhaqi in *Shu'ab al-Iman* through Abi Umama, Anas, and Abu Mas'ud al-Ansari, and by al-Hakim in his *Mustadrak* from the latter. Al-Shafi'i in his *Musnad* relates the first

It was narrated by Ibn Majah and al-Tabarani in *al-Kabir*. What is understood from his words "His invocation is shown to me until he finishes it" is that no sooner does the person invoking blessings begin invoking them that the Prophet 🕌 hears them until he finishes.

The questioner did well to see clarification from the Prophet – blessings and peace upon him, his Family, and his Companions – when he asked him: "Even after death?" wherefore the Prophet 🕌 made it clear that such disclosure does take place after death, because of the existence of the attribute of life in such disclosure. Then he made it even clearer and more explicit, saying: "Therefore Allah's Prophet is alive!" He thus characterized Prophets as being alive; but he did not stop there. He went on to say: "and sustained," as sustenance is the greatest separator between the living and the non-living. In this way the Prophet 🕌 did not leave any ambiguity on the issue except he dispelled it. May Allah reward the questioner on behalf of all Muslims!

4. Al-Bayhaqi also mentioned the Prophet's 🕌 hadith from Aws ibn Aws whereby the Prophet 🕌 said: "Your best day is the day of *Jum'a*. On it Adam was created, and on it his soul was taken back, and on it will the final trumpet-blast take place, and on it will the great Thunderstrike *(al-sa'qa)* take place. Therefore invoke blessings upon me abundantly on that day, for your invocation is shown to me." They said: "O Messenger of Allah! How will our invocation be shown to you after you have turned to dust?" He said: "Verily, Allah has forbidden the earth from eating the

---

part only ("Invoke blessings upon me abundantly on Friday") *mursal* from Safwan ibn Salim.

bodies of Prophets!" *(Afdalu ayyâmikum yawmu al-jumu'ati fîhi khuliqa Âdamu wa fîhi al-nafkhatu wa fîhi al-sa'qatu fa akthirû 'alayya min al-salâti fa inna salâtakum ma'rûdatun 'alayya. Qâlû yâ Rasûlallâhi wa kayfa tu'radu salâtuna 'alayka wa qad aramta? Qâla inna Allâha* 🕮 *harrama 'alâ al-arda an ta'kula ajsâda al-anbiyâ'.)* [39]

It was narrated by Abu Dawud, Ibn Majah, Ibn Hibban in his *Sahih*, and al-Hakim who declared it *sahîh*. Al-Bayhaqi cited textual witnesses for it, then he narrated the hadith: "Verily, Allah has angels that roam the earth and convey to me the greeting of my Community."[40] He cited other hadiths as well.[41]

The above hadith from Aws is sound *(sahîh)* and strengthens the previous hadith narrated by Ibn Majah and al-

---

[39]Narrated from Aws ibn Aws al-Thaqafi by Ahmad in his *Musnad* with a sound chain according to al-Zayn (12:474 #16107), Ibn Abi Shayba in his *Musannaf* (2:516), Abu Dawud, al-Nasa'i, Ibn Majah, al-Darimi in his *Musnad* with a sound chain as stated by Shaykh Husayn Asad, Abu Nu'aym in *Ma'rifa al-Sahaba* (#976), Ibn Khuzayma in his *Sahih* with a sound chain according to al-A'zami (3:118 #1733), Ibn Hibban with a sound chain by Muslim's criterion according to Shu'ayb al-Arna'ut (3:190-191 #910), al-Hakim *(sahîh,* confirmed by al-Dhahabi 1:278, 4:560=1990 ed. 1:413, 4:604), al-Qadi Isma'il in *Fadl al-Salat* with a sound chain according to al-Albani (p. 35), al-Tabarani in his *Kabir* (1:216 #589), al-Bayhaqi in his *Sunan* (3:248), *Shu'ab al-Iman* (3:109-110), and *Fada'il al-Awqat* (p. 497), and Ibn al-Qayyim who declared its chain *"sahîh* without doubt" in *Jala' al-Afham* (p. 66-74=42-48). As'ad Tayyim alone weakened Aws's narration and went so far as to declare it *munkar* in *Takhrij Hadith Aws al-Thaqafi* (p. 5-66) which follows his *Bayan Awham al-Albani.* Also narrated with the wording: "Verily, among your best days is the day of *Jum'a" (inna min afdali ayyamikum yawma al-jumu'a).* Cf. Ibn Hajar in *Fath al-Bari* (1989 ed. 6:379=1959 ed. 6:488).
[40]See below, n. 60.
[41]In *Hayat al-Anbiya' fî Quburihim.*

23

Tabarani with regard to the disclosure of the invocation of blessings to the Prophet 🌿 and the non-consumption by the earth of
the bodies of Prophets.

> 5. From Anas 🌿: "Prophets are not left in their graves
>   beyond forty nights but [thereafter] stand in prayer
>   before Allah until the Trumpet-Blast." *(Al-anbiyâ'u lâ
>   yutrakûna fî qubûrihim ba'da arba'îna laylatan wa
>   lâkin yusallûna bayna yaday Allâhi hattâ yunfakhu fî
>   al-sûr.)* [42]

---

[42]Narrated from Anas by al-Hakim in his *Tarikh* and his student al-
Bayhaqi in *Hayat al-Anbiya'* as well as al-Tabarani in *Musnad al-
Shamiyyin* (1:196, 2:420) and Abu Nu'aym in *Hilya al-Awliya* (1985
ed. 8:333), the latter two with weak chains containing al-Hasan ibn
Yahya al-Khushani [see Arna'ut and Ma'ruf, *al-Tahrir* (1:282-283
#1295)]. Ibn Hajar in *Fath al-Bari* (1959 ed. 6:487) and *Talkhis al-
Habir* (2:125) suggests that its rank is *hasan* based on corroborative
narrations adduced by al-Bayhaqi. Al-Suyuti explicitly declares it
hasan in his discussion of the hadith in *al-La'ali' al-Masnu'a* (1996 ed.
1:260=1981 ed. 1:284) with the wording: "No Prophet dies and resides
in his grave for forty mornings except his soul is given back to him."
Both al-Suyuti in *al-Ta'aqqubat* (p. 53) and Ibn Hajar reject Ibn al-
Jawzi's and Ibn Hibban's verdicts – respectively in *al-Mawdu'at*
(1:303) and *al-Majruhin* (1:235) – that the two wordings are forged, as
related by al-Munawi in *Fayd al-Qadir*. Furthermore, the chains
adduced by Ibn al-Jawzi and Ibn Hibban are merely weak because of
al-Hasan ibn Yahya al-Khushani, as stated above.

'Abd al-Razzaq in his *Musannaf* (3:576) further narrates from
Sa'id ibn al-Musayyib that he said: "No Prophet is left on the earth
beyond forty days [after his death]." Ibn Hajar declares it weak in
Talkhis al-Habir (2:125), pointing out that 'Abd al-Razzaq follows it
up with the hadith of Musa's 🌿 standing in his grave in prayer [see
hadith #6 below] while al-Shawkani correctly considers it precluded by
the sound narrations of the Prophets' life in the grave in *Nayl al-Awtar*,
chapter on visiting the Prophet 🌿. See also Ibn al-Mulaqqin, *Khulasa
al-Badr al-Munir* (1:267).

Al-Hakim narrated it in his *Tarikh* and al-Bayhaqi in his *Sunan*. The latter said: "If it is sound *(sahîh)* in this wording, the meaning is – and Allah knows best – that by the words 'they are not left' is meant that they do not pray [in the grave] except for that length of time, after which they pray before Allah directly."

    1a. Ibn 'Adi in his *al-Kamil fi al-Du'afa'* narrated from Thabit, from Anas, that the Prophet 鷺 said: "The Prophets are alive in their grave, praying."[43] Abu Ya'la also narrated it with trustworthy narrators. So did al-Bayhaqi, and he declared this hadith sound. It is sounder than the previous one.

    6. Our Prophet – Allah's blessings and peace upon him and his Family and Companions – had passed, on his Night Journey, by Musa 鷺 as the latter was standing in his grave, praying. The Prophet 鷺 said: "I passed, on my Night Journey, by Musa at the red dune as he was standing in prayer in his grave." *(Marartu bi Mûsa laylata usrya bî inda al-kathîbi al-ahmari wa huwa qâ'imun yusallî fî qabrihi.)*[44]

It is narrated by Ibn 'Asakir, al-Tabarani, al-Nasa'i, Ibn Hibban, Ibn Khuzayma, and Muslim. From this hadith the meaning of the former [#5] narration can be understood in the sense that the Prophets are not left in their grave without prayer; rather, they stand in their prayer before Allah, adamant to the

---

[43]See n. 29.

[44]Narrated from Anas by Muslim, al-Nasa'i both in his *Sunan* and *al-Sunan al-Kubra* (1:419), Ahmad, Ibn Khuzayma in his *Sahih*, Ibn Hibban in his (1:242), Abu Yala in his *Musnad* (6:71), 'Abd ibn Hamid in his, Ibn Abi Shayba in his *Musannaf* (7:335), Ibn Marduyah, and al-Bayhaqi in *Hayat al-Anbiya'*; also from other Companions but with very weak chains as indicated by al-Haythami in *Majma' al-Zawa'id* (8:205).

grave and to all things other than Allah, immersed in their contemplation and the delight of *salât* which was made the apple of the Prophet's 🕌 eyes in this world.

7. It is established that the Prophet 🕌 gathered with all the Prophets at the Far Mosque in the Holy Sanctuary and they were alive and endowed with their human forms. The Prophet 🕌 led them in prayer and they prayed behind him, taking him as their imam. The Prophet 🕌 said: "You could have seen me in the assembly of the Prophets. There was Musa عليه السلام standing in prayer, a tall man with curly hair who resembles the tribesmen of Shanu'a. There was 'Isa ibn Maryam عليه السلام standing in prayer; closest to him in resemblance is 'Urwa ibn Mas'ud al-Thaqafi.[45] There was Ibrahim عليه السلام standing in prayer. The closest of people in resemblance to him is your Companion" – meaning himself. "Then it was time for prayer, so I led them in prayer." *(Wa qad ra'aytanî fî jamâ'atin min al-anbyâ'i fa'idhâ Mûsâ عليه السلام qâ'imun yusallî fa'idhâ rajulun darbun ja'dun ka'annahu min rijâli shanû'ata wa idhâ 'Îsâ ibnu Maryama عليه السلام qâ'imun yusallî aqrabu al-nâsi bihi shabahan 'Urwatu ibnu Mas'ûdin al-Thaqafî wa idhâ Ibrâhîmu عليه السلام qâ'imun yusallî ashbahu al-nâsi bihi sâhibukum – ya'nî nafsahu – fahânat al-salâtu fa amamtuhum.)* [46]

---

[45]On 'Urwa see n. 110.
[46]Narrated from Abu Hurayra by Muslim as part of a longer hadith. Ahmad narrates it also from Abu Hurayra but without mention of the Prophet's 🕌 imamate. Al-Tirmidhi narrates it *(hasan sahîh gharîb)* from Jabir without mention of the Prophet's 🕌 imamate, but adding the likening of Gibrîl عليه السلام to Dihya ibn Khalifa al-Kalbi, as he does in his *Shama'il* (p. 40).

Muslim narrated it. The Prophet's 攤 words "then it was time for prayer" shows that they keep watch of prayer-times and observe prayers on time. In recapitulation: the Prophet 攤 saw them praying in their graves on his Night Journey; then he saw them in the Farthest Mosque; then he saw them in the various heavens – all at that same time and according to their levels, from the first heaven to the seventh – when he was taken up in his ascension. At that time he met Musa 攤 in the sixth heaven. That is why Allah said: ❨**We verily gave Musa the Scripture; so be not in doubt of meeting him**❩ (32:23), that is: on the night of the Ascension, as the scholars of Qur'anic commentary have stated.[47]

8. It is also established that the Prophet – blessings and peace upon him and his Family and Companions – saw Musa 攤, 'Isa 攤, and Ibrahim 攤 circumambulating the Ka'ba.[48]

9. He described Musa 攤 as a tall wavy-haired man who resembled the tribesmen of Azd Shanu'a, and 'Isa 攤 as a medium-built man who looked [fair and bright] as if he had just come out of a bath *(dîmâs)*.

---

[47]Narrated with a sound chain from Ibn 'Abbas and Qatada by al-Diya' al-Maqdisi in *al-Mukhtara* as stated by al-Suyuti in *al-Durr al-Manthur* (6:555-556); and by Ibn Abi Hatim, Ibn Marduya, Mujahid (2:511), al-Tabari (21:112), Ibn Kathir (3:464), al-Qurtubi (14:108), al-Tha'alibi (3:216), al-Wahidi (2:855), Ibn al-Jawzi (6:343), al-Nahhas (5:311), al-Shawkani (4:256) and others in their *Tafsirs* of the verse.
[48]For Ibrahim 攤 [sitting against the Ka'ba rather than circumambu-lating it]: hadith of the Prophet 攤 on the *Bayt al-Ma'mûr* narrated from Malik ibn Sa'sa'a by Bukhari, Muslim, and Ahmad, and from Anas by Muslim and Ahmad. For Musa 攤: see below, #11-13. For 'Isa 攤: see below, n. 50.

He described himself as being the closest to Ibrahim
علیه السلام in resemblance.[49]

10. Al-Tirmidhi in the *Shama'il* narrated that the Prophet
ﷺ saw 'Isa علیه السلام with his head dripping water after he
had showered with Zamwam water, and likened him
to 'Urwa ibn Mas'ud رضی الله عنه.[50]

11. He ﷺ said: "I can see Musa in this valley [Mecca] in
pilgrim's garb, wearing two short white cotton
drapes." *(Ka'annî anzuru ilâ Mûsâ ibni 'Imrâna fî
hâdhâ al-wâdî muhriman bayna qutwâniyyatayn.)*[51]

Al-Tabarani narrated it.

12. Another version narrated by Ahmad, Muslim, and Ibn
Majah states: "He had a loud shout *(ju'âr)*." That is,

---

[49]Narrated from Abu Hurayra by Bukhari, Muslim, al-Tirmidhi *(hasan
sahîh)*, and Ahmad.

[50]I did not find this in al-Tirmidhi's *Shama'il* nor in his *Sunan*, however, the Prophet ﷺ did describe 'Isa علیه السلام as "having the most beautiful
hair you could have seen, wavy, shoulder-length and dripping with
water, resting his hands on the shoulders of two men, circumambulating the House." Narrated from Ibn 'Umar by Bukhari in three places,
Muslim in two, Ahmad, and Malik in his *Muwatta'*. His likeness to
'Urwa ibn Mas'ud is mentioned in the Prophet's ﷺ narrations from
Jabir, Abu Hurayra, and 'Abd Allah ibn 'Amr by Muslim and Ahmad,
and from Jabir by al-Tirmidhi *(hasan sahîh gharîb)*.

[51]Narrated from Ibn Mas'ud by Abu Ya'la in his *Musnad* (9:27) and al-
Tabarani in *al-Awsat* (6:307-308) and *al-Kabir* (10:142) with a chain
stated fair one time and weak another by al-Haythami in *Majma' al-
Zawa'id* (8:204, 3:221) because of Yazid ibn Sinan Abu Farwa al-
Ruhawi, whose grade varies from "passable" *(muqârib, sâlih)*
according to Bukhari and Ibn 'Adi, to "discarded" according to al-
Nasa'i and al-Azdi, while Ibn Hajar grades him "weak" *(da'îf)* in his
Taqrib, a grade confirmed by al-Arna'ut and Ma'ruf in *Tahrir al-
Taqrib* (4:112 #7727).

he raised his voice in proffering service *(talbiya)* and other [formulas of submission and supplication]. *(Ka'annî anzuru ilâ Mûsâ hâbitan min al-thaniyyati wa lahu ju'ârun ilallâhi bi al-talbiyati.)* [52]

13. It is also established that the Prophet ﷺ saw Yunus عليه السلام performing pilgrimage, as he had emerged from the hill, shouting the *talbiya*. The Prophet ﷺ said: "I can see Yunus ibn Matta عليه السلام riding a red she-camel and wearing a woolen cloak, clutching the halter of his camel and shouting the *talbiya*." *(Ka'annî anzuru ilâ Yûnus ibni Mattâ 'alâ nâqatin hamrâ'a ja'datin 'alayhi jubbatun min sûfin khitâmu nâqatihi khulbatun wa huwa yulabbî.)* [53]

Ahmad and Muslim narrated it.

II.   Commentary and Further Proof-Texts

Does anyone doubt that the Prophets are alive after hearing the foregoing evidence which consists in sound *(sahîh)* narrations? Does their prayer, circumambulation, ritual showering, pilgrimage, *talbiya*, shouting, wearing of a woolen cloak, riding on a camel, and receiving sustenance in the grave, undecaying and impassible bodies, all consist in baseless imaginings? [54] Further, can any of these matters – such as prayer, cir-

---

[52]Hadith of the Prophet ﷺ: "I can see *(ka'annî anzuru)* Musa عليه السلام descending from high ground, shouting with power unto Allah with his *talbiya*... I can see Yunus ibn Matta," etc. Narrated from Ibn 'Abbas by Muslim in two places, Ibn Majah, and Ahmad.

[53]Same hadith as #12.

[54]For sound reports from Jabir ibn 'Abd Allah ﷺ on the impassibility of the martyrs of Uhud in their graves see Ibn 'Abd al-Barr, *al-Tamhid* (18:174).

cumambulation, showering, and other acts that were mentioned
such as camel-riding and sustenance in the grave – can they be
attributed to souls devoid of bodies? The dead are incapable of
experiencing such states, while souls are not in need of such
matters. Therefore, it is indispensable that both bodies and souls
be reunited in the persons of the Prophets – Allah's blessings
and peace upon them! What further indicates that they are alive
is that the Prophet ﷺ described Ibrahim عليه السلام, Musa عليه السلام, and
Yunus عليه السلام, when he met with them, in the same terms in which
he described 'Isa عليه السلام with regard to life, without adding anything: and 'Isa's life is established by both the text *(al-nass)* and
the Consensus *(al-ijmâ')*.[55]

There is no difference, therefore, between the [current]
life of the Prophets and that of 'Isa عليه السلام. It follows that no-one
denies the lives of the Prophets – upon them Allah's blessings
and peace! – and the impassivity of their bodies except those
who possess no knowledge of the Book and the Sunna. The
latter have no inkling of the immense rank of Prophets and the
merits which Allah has bestowed specifically upon them, distin-
guishing them above the rest of human beings. Indeed, Allah ﷻ
forbade us to call "dead" whoever is killed for Allah's sake
❪Nay! They live, finding their sustenance in the presence of
their lord❫ (3:169). The Prophets, therefore, are even more
deserving and meriting of that. For the martyrs do not reach the
rank of Prophets, nor did they reach the rank of martyrs except

---

[55]On the position of *Ahl al-Sunna* on the life of 'Isa عليه السلام see Ibn Kathir,
Tafsir (1981 Dar al-Fikr ed. 1:578 for verse 4:159), al-Nawawi, *Sharh
Sahih Muslim* (1972 ed. 2:234), Ibn Hajar, *Fath al-Bari* (1959 ed.
6:375), al-Shawkani's epistle entitled *al-Tawdih fi Tawatur Ma Ja'a fi
al-Ahadith fi al-Mahdi wa al-Dajjal wa al-Masih*, al-'Azim Abadi,
'Awn al-Ma'bud (11:308-313), and Shaykh 'Abd Allah al-Ghumari's
forty hadiths entitled *'Aqida Ahl al-Islam fi Nuzul 'Isa 'Alayhi al-
Salam*. The latter two texts were compiled in refutation of the heresy of
the pseudo-prophet of Qadyan, Ahmad Ghulam.

through the blessing of earnestly following the Prophets –
Allah's blessings and peace upon them! The martyrs are but one
of the merits of Prophets, and they are also below the Truthful
and Trusting Saints *(al-Siddîqîn)* in level.

Furthermore, there is no problem in the Prophet's 鐺
sight of the Prophets praying in their graves, then his sighting
them in the Farthest Mosque, then in the different heavens at that
same time. After death, the field belongs to the souls, and the
actions of souls cannot be judged by the minds. Bodies, after
death, are subservient to souls, and the latter are subtle entities;
just as in the world, souls are subservient to bodies which are
dense entities.

Al-Bayhaqi said: "There are [other] textual witnesses to
the life of the Prophets – Allah's blessings and peace upon them!
– among the sound narrations." He then mentioned the hadith: "I
passed by Musa as he was standing in his grave, praying"[56] and
other narrations that state the Prophet's 鐺 meeting with other
Prophets, including the hadith of the two *Sahih*s:

14. Do not say that I am better *(lâ tukhayyirûnî)* than
    Musa, for on the Day of Resurrection human beings
    shall all fall unconscious *(yus'aqûn)* and I shall fall
    unconscious with them; then I shall be the first to
    regain consciousness, and lo! there will be Musa,
    firmly grasping the side of the Throne. I do not know
    whether he was among those who fell unconscious
    and got up before me, or whether he was among those
    whom Allah exempted. *(Lâ tukhayyirûnî 'alâ Mûsâ
    fa'inna al-nâsa yus'aqûna yawma al-qiyâmati fa
    as'aqu ma'ahum fa akûnu awwala man yufîqu fa idhâ
    Mûsâ bâtishun jâniba al-'arshi fa lâ adrî akâna fî*

---

[56]See above, #6 and n. 44 (p. 25).

man sa'iqa fa afâqa aw kâna mimman istathnâ Allâh.) [57]

Al-Bayhaqi said: "The above event can only be true provided that Allah returns the souls of Prophets to them after death so that they are **⟨living in the presence of their lord⟩** (3:169) as the martyrs are, so that when the trumpet is blown the first time, every living being will fall unconscious, and they will also fall unconscious. However, this state is not identical with death in the full sense but only in the sense of losing all one's senses at that particular time.

It is also said that the martyrs are among those Allah 🕮 exempts according to His saying: **⟨save him whom Allah wills⟩** in the verse **⟨And the Day when the Trumpet will be blown, and all who are in the heavens and the earth will start in fear, save him whom Allah wills⟩** (27:87).[58] And where do the martyrs stand in comparison with the Prophets?

Al-Samhudi said – may Allah have mercy upon him – that among the evidence supporting the fact that the Prophets are alive – Allah's blessings and peace upon them – is the following narration of the Prophet 🕮:

---

[57]Narrated from Abu Hurayra by Bukhari in three places, Muslim, Abu Dawud, al-Tirmidhi *(hasan sahîh)*, and Ahmad.

[58]Narrated from Abu Hurayra and Ibn 'Abbas by Sa'id ibn Mansur, al-Tabari in his *Tafsir* (17:110, 20:19-20, 24:20), 'Abd ibn Hamid, 'Ali ibn Sa'id in *al-Ta'a wa al-'Isyan*, Abu Ya'la in his *Musnad*, Ibn al-Mundhir, al-Qattan in his *Mutawwalat*, al-Tabarani in his, Abu Musa al-Madini in his, Ibn Abi Hatim, Abu al-Shaykh in *al-'Azama*, and al-Bayhaqi in *al-Ba'th wa al-Nushur* as compiled by al-Suyuti in *al-Durr al-Manthur* (6:384, 7:256). Also narrated from Ibn 'Abbas by Ibn Kathir (2:147, 3:205, 3:378), al-Qurtubi (13:241, also in *al-Tadhkira*), al-Tha'alibi (3:70), Ibn al-Jawzi (6:195), al-Shawkani (4:155), and al-Nahhas (5:149).

15. "Verily, 'Isa ibn Maryam عليه السلام shall descend and pass through al- Madina on his way to pilgrimage, and if he greets me I shall certainly answer him!" Its actual wording is: "Verily, Ibn Maryam عليه السلام shall descend, an equitable judge and a fair ruler. He shall tread his path on his way to pilgrimage and come to my grave to greet me, and I shall certainly answer him!" *(Layahbitunna Ibnu Maryama hakaman 'adlan wa imâman muqsitan wa layaslukunna fajjan hâjjan aw mu'tamiran wa laya'tiyunna qabrî hattâ yusallima 'alayya wa la'aruddunna 'alayh.)* [59] See also below [**#22**].

III.   The Special Life of Our Prophet ﷺ

It is established that our Prophet ﷺ possesses an isthmus-life that is greater and more perfect than that of any other, of which he himself told us. It is equally established that he is intimately connected with the Community, fully cognizant of their states, seeing their actions, hearing their speech, replying to their greetings, and the hadiths to that effect are numerous.

16. Among these hadiths is the narration of the Prophet ﷺ from 'Abd Allah ibn Mas'ud رضي الله عنه: "Verily, Allah has angels that roam the earth and convey to me the greeting of my Community." *(Inna lillâhi malâ'ikatan sayyâhîna fî al-ardi yuballighûnî min ummatî al-salâm.)* [60]

---

[59]Narrated from Abu Hurayra by al-Hakim who declared it sound (1990 ed. 2:651 #4162), and al-Dhahabi concurred.

[60]Narrated from Ibn Mas'ud with a sound chain by Muslim's criterion as stated by Shaykh Shu'ayb Arna'ut in Ibn Hibban's *Sahih* (3:195 #914), al-'Azim Abadi in *'Awn al-Ma'bud* (6:21), Ibn al-Qayyim who declared its chain sound in *Jala' al-Afham* (p. 24), and al-Hakim in *al-*

Al-Mundhiri said: "Al-Nasa'i and Ibn Hibban in his *Sahih* narrated it." Isma'il al-Qadi[61] and others have narrated it through various paths with chains that leave no doubt as to their soundness. All of these chains are to Sufyan al-Thawri: From 'Abd Allah ibn al-Sa'ib: From Zadhan: From 'Abd Allah ibn Mas'ud. Al-Thawri explicitly declared having heard it from 'Abd Allah ibn al-Sa'ib, as reported in al-Qadi Isma'il's book. As for 'Abd Allah ibn al-Sa'ib and Zadhan, Muslim used them as sub-narrators [in his *Sahih*], and Ibn Ma'in declared them trustworthy *(thiqa)*, so the chain is sound.[62]

Mustadrak, confirmed by al-Dhahabi (2:241=1990 ed. 2:456). Also narrated by al-Nasa'i with six chains in his *Sunan*, *al-Sunan al-Kubra* (3:43), and *'Amal al-Yawm wa al-Layla* (2:167), Isma'il al-Qadi in *Fadl al-Salat 'ala al-Nabi* 🕮 (p. 34), al-Bayhaqi in *Shu'ab al-Iman* (2:217) and *al-Sunan al-Kubra* (1:380), Abu Ya'la in his *Musnad* (9:137 #5213), Ahmad in his, al-Darimi in his, Ibn Abi Shayba in his *Musannaf* (2:253=2:517, 6:316), 'Abd al-Razzaq in his (2:215 #3116), al-Tabarani in *al-Kabir* (#10528-10530), Ibn al-Mubarak in *al-Zuhd* (p. 364 #1028) and his *Musnad* (p. 30 #51), and al-Khatib in *Talkhis al-Mutashabih* (p. 766).

[61]The Imam and hadith master, *Shaykh al-Islam* Abu Ishaq Isma'il ibn Ishaq ibn Isma'il ibn Hammad ibn Zayd al-Azdi Jahdami al-Qadi al-Maliki (199-282), author of several works, including a *Musnad*. See al-Dhahabi, *Siyar* (Arna'ut ed. 13:341).

[62]Zadhan in this narration is Abu 'Umar al-Kindi al-Bazzaz as named explicitly in Abu Sa'id al-Shashi's (d. 335) narration of this hadith in his *Musnad* (2:252). Muslim narrated from him, from Ibn 'Umar, two narrations of the Prophet 🕮 in three places: "Whoever strikes his slave in the face or beats him unjustly, his expiation is to manumit him," and the Prophet's 🕮 prohibition of the use of wine fermentation-vessels. See also Abu Bakr al-Asbahani's *Rijal Muslim* (1:230) and Ibn Hajar's *Taqrib*. He was declared *thiqa* by Ibn Ma'in, Ibn Sa'd, al-'Ijli, Ibn Shahin, al-Khatib, and al-Dhahabi as reported by Arna'ut and Ma'ruf in *al-Tahrir* (1:409 #1976). From 'Abd Allah ibn al-Sa'ib al-Kindi or al-Shaybani al-Kufi, Muslim narrated through two chains the hadith of Thabit ibn al-Dahhak whereby the Prophet 🕮 forbade sharecropping. He is trustworthy *(thiqa)* as stated in Ibn Hajar's *Taqrib* (1:304 #3339).

17. Also among these hadiths is Ibn Mas'ud's narration
that the Prophet ﷺ said: "My life is a great good for
you, you will relate about me and it will be related to
you, and my death is a great good for you, your
actions will be presented to me, and if I see goodness I
will praise Allah, and if I see evil I will ask
forgiveness of Him for you." *(Hayâtî khayrun lakum
tuhaddithûna wa yuhaddathu lakum wa wafâtî
khayrun lakum tu'radu a'malukum 'alayya famâ
ra'aytu min khayrin hamidtu Allâha wa mâ ra'aytu
min sharrin istaghfartu Allâha lakum.)* [63]

The rest of the sub-narrators of this hadith are all the men of Bukhari
and Muslim.
[63]Narrated from Ibn Mas'ud by al-Bazzar in his *Musnad* (1:397) with a
sound chain as stated by al-Suyuti in *Manahil al-Safa* (p. 31 #8) and *al-
Khasa'is al-Kubra* (2:281), al-Haythami in *Majma' al-Zawa'id* (9:24
#91), and al-'Iraqi in *Tarh al-Tathrib* (3:297) – his last book, as
opposed to *al-Mughni'an Haml al-Asfar* (4:148) where he questions
the trustworthy rank of one of the narrators in al-Bazzar's chain.
Shaykh 'Abd Allah al-Talidi said in his *Tahdhib al-Khasa'is al-Kubra*
(p. 458-459 #694) that this chain is sound according to Muslim's
criterion and Shaykh Mahmud Mamduh in *Raf'al-Minara* (p. 156-169)
discussed it at length and declared it sound. Their shaykh, al-Sayyid
'Abd Allah ibn al-Siddiq al-Ghumari declared it sound in his
monograph *Nihaya al-Amal fi Sharh wa Tashih Hadith 'Ard al-A'mal.*
Opposing these six judgments al-Albani declares it weak in his notes
on al-Qadi Isma'il's *Fadl al-Salat* (p. 37 n. 1). It is also narrated with
weak chains from Anas and – with two sound *mursal* chains missing
the Companion-link – from the Successor Bakr ibn 'Abd Allah al-
Muzani by Isma'il al-Qadi (d. 282) in his *Fadl al-Salat 'ala al-Nabi* ﷺ
(p. 36-39 #25-26). The latter chain was declared sound by al-Qari in
Sharh al-Shifa' (1:102), Shaykh al-Islam al-Taqi al-Subki in *Shifa' al-
Siqam*, his critic Ibn 'Abd al-Hadi in *al-Sarim al-Munki* (p. 217), and
al-Albani in his *Silsila Da'ifa* (2:405). A third, weak chain is related
from Bakr al-Muzani by al-Harith ibn Abi Usama (d. 282) in his
Musnad (2:884) as per Ibn Hajar in *al-Matalib al-'Aliya* (4:23). Al-
Albani declared the hadith weak on the grounds that some authorities

questioned the memorization of the *Murji'* hadith master 'Abd al-Majid ibn 'Abd al-'Aziz ibn Abi Rawwad. However, he was retained by Muslim in his *Sahih* and declared *thiqa* by Yahya ibn Ma'in, Ahmad, Abu Dawud, al-Nasa'i, Ibn Shahin, al-Khalili, and al-Daraqutni, while al-Dhahabi listed him in *Man Tukullima Fihi Wa Huwa Muwaththaq* (p. 124) as stated by Mamduh in *Raf' al-Minara* (p. 163, 167). Al-Arna'ut and Ma'ruf declare him *thiqa* in *Tahrir al-Taqrib* (2:379 #4160) as well as Dr. Nur al-Din 'Itr in his edition of al-Dhahabi's *Mughni* (1:571 #3793) and Dr. Khaldun al-Ahdab in *Zawa'id Tarikh Baghdad* (10:464). Even if al-Albani's grading were hypothetically accepted, then the weak *musnad* narration in conjunction with the sound *mursal* one – graded *sahih* by al-Albani – would yield a final grading of *hasan* or *sahih*, not *da'if*. In addition to this, Mamduh quoted al-Albani's own words in the latter's attempted refutation of Shaykh Isma'il al-Ansari entitled *Kitab al-Shaybani* (1:134-135) whereby "The sound *mursal* hadith is a proof in all Four Schools and other than them among the imams of the principles of hadith and *fiqh*, therefore it is apparent to every fair-minded person that the position whereby such a hadith does not form a proof only because it is *mursal*, is untenable." This is one of many examples in which al-Albani not only contradicts, but soundly refutes himself.

Shaykh Hasanayn Muhammad Makhluf wrote in his *Fatawa Shar'iyya* (1:91-92): "The hadith means that the Prophet ﷺ is a great good for his Community during his life, because Allah the Exalted has preserved the Community, through the secret of the Prophet's ﷺ presence, from misguidance, confusion, and disagreement, and He has guided the people through the Prophet ﷺ to the manifest truth; and that after Allah took back the Prophet ﷺ, our connection to the latter's goodness continues uncut and the extension of his goodness endures, overshadowing us. The deeds of the Community are shown to him every day, and he glorifies Allah for the goodness that he finds, while he asks for His forgiveness for the small sins, and the alleviation of His punishment for the grave ones: and this is a tremendous good for us. There is therefore 'goodness for the Community in his life, and in his death, goodness for the Community.' Moreover, as has been established in the hadith, the Prophet ﷺ is alive in his grave with a special 'isthmus-life' stronger than the lives of the martyrs which the Qur'an spoke of in more than one verse. The nature of these two kinds of life cannot be known except by their Bestower, the Glorious, the Exalted. He is able to do all things. His showing the Community's

The hadith master al-'Iraqi said in the book of *Jana'iz* of his work *Tarh al-Tathrib fi Sharh al-Taqrib*: "Its chain is good" *(isnâduhu jayyid).*[64] The hadith master al-Haythami said: "Al-Bazzar narrated it and its sub-narrators are the men of the *Sahih.*"[65] The hadith master al-Suyuti declared it sound *(sahîh)* in *al-Mu'jizat* and *al-Khasa'is.* So did al-Qastallani the commentator of al-Bukhari. Al-Munawi also declared, in *Fayd al-Qadir,* that it is *sahîh.*[66] So did al-Zurqani in his commentary on al-Qastallani's *al-Mawahib al-Laduniyya.* So did Shihab al-Din al-Khafaji in his commentary on [al-Qadi 'Iyad's] *al-Shifa'.*[67] So did al-Mulla 'Ali al-Qari in his, adding: "Al-Harith ibn Usama narrated it in his *Musnad* with a sound chain."[68] Ibn Hajar also mentioned it in *al-Matalib al-'Alya.*[69] This hadith also came to us through another, *mursal* way from [the *Tabi'î*] Bakr ibn 'Abd Allah al-Muzani. The hadith master Isma'il al-Qadi narrated it in his monograph on the invocation of blessings on the Prophet ﷺ,

---

deeds to the Prophet ﷺ as an honorific gift for him and his Community is entirely possible rationally and documented in the reports. There is no leeway for its denial; and Allah guides to His light whomever He pleases; and Allah knows best."

[64] Al-'Iraqi, *Tarh al-Tathrib* (3:297).

[65] Al-Haythami, *Majma' al-Zawa'id* (9:24 #91).

[66] Al-Munawi in *Fayd al-Qadir* (3:401) only reported al-'Iraqi's words "Its narrators are the men of the *Sahih* except for 'Abd al-Majid ibn Abi Rawwad who, despite being retained by Muslim as a narrator and being declared trustworthy *(thiqa)* by Ibn Ma'in and al-Nasa'i, was declared weak by some." Al-Munawi then went on to criticize al-Suyuti's unmitigated authentication of the narration in *Manahil al-Safa* although al-Suyuti is correct.

[67] Al-Khafaji, *Sharh al-Shifa'* (1:102).

[68] Al-Qari, *Sharh al-Shifa'* (1:102), referring to the *mursal* hadith of Bakr al-Muzani.

[69] Ibn Hajar, *al-Matalib al-'Alya* (4:22).

and Shaykh al-Albani said about it: "*Mursal sahîh.*"[70] The hadith master Ibn 'Abd al-Hadi declared it sound *(sahîh)* despite his excessive rigor and harshness in his book *al-Sarim al-Munki*. After all this evidence, does any meddler have anything left to say? The hadith is undoubtedly sound, and no-one questions its authenticity.

This hadith indicates that the Prophet ﷺ knows about our actions because they are being shown to him, and he asks Allah forgiveness on our behalf for whatever wrong we may do. If this is the case, then it is permissible for us to use him as a means to Allah and ask for his intercession with Him. For he knows our case, and so he can intercede for us and supplicate for us, as he is the intercesor whose intercession is granted – may Allah send blessings and peace upon him and his Family, and increase him in honor and bounty.

Allah has informed us in the Qur'an that the Prophet ﷺ is a witness over his entire Community. This assuredly requires that the actions of his Community be shown to him so that he may witness to whatever he saw and knew:

> **18.** Ibn al-Mubarak said: One of the *Ansâr* narrated to us from al-Minhal ibn 'Amr that the latter hears Sa'id ibn al-Musayyib say: "Not one day passes except the Prophet's ﷺ Community is shown to him morning and evening. He knows them by their marks [or names] and their actions, thereby giving witness concerning them. Allah said: ❴**But how (will it be with them) when we bring of every people a witness, and We bring you (O Muhammad) a**

---

[70]In his edition of Isma'il al-Qadi's *Fadl al-Salat 'ala al-Nabi* ﷺ (p. 37), after which he goes on to say that the hadith is weak, as in his *Silsila Da'ifa* (#979).

witness against these? (4:41). *(Laysa min yawmin illâ wa yu'radu fîhi 'alâ al-nabiyyi* ﷺ *ummatuhu ghuduwwatan wa 'ashiyyan fa ya'rifuhum bi sîmâhum wa a'mâlihim fa lidhâlika yashhadu 'alayhim. Yaqûlu Allâhu ta'âlâ...)* [71]

19. Also among these hadiths is the narration from 'Ammar ibn Yassir ﷺ that the Prophet ﷺ said: "Verily, Allah has put an angel in charge of my grave and given him the names of all creatures. No-one invokes blessings upon me until the Day of Resurrection except he informs me of his name and the name of his father thus: So-and-so son of So-and-so has just invoked blessings upon you." *(Inna Allâha wakkala bi qabrî malakan a'tâhu Allâhu asmâ'a al-khalâ'iqi falâ yusallî 'alayya ahadun ilâ yawmi al-qiyâmati illâ ablaghanî bi ismihi wa ismi abîhi hâdhâ fulânu ibnu fulânin qad sallâ 'alayk.)*

It is narrated by al-Bazzar, while Abu al-Shaykh – Ibn Hayyan – narrates it thus:

20. The Prophet ﷺ said: "Allah ﷺ has an angel to whom he has given the names of all creatures, and he shall stand at my grave, after I die, so that none shall invoke blessings upon me except he shall say: 'O Muhammad, So-and-so son of So-and-so has just invoked blessings upon you.' Thereupon the Almighty Lord shall send a blessing upon that person, tenfold for each blessing he invoked upon me." *(Inna lillâhi*

---

[71]Narrated by Ibn al-Mubarak in *al-Zuhd* (p. 42), Ibn Kathir *(asmâ'ihim* instead of *sîmâhum)* in his *Tafsir* (1:500), al-Qurtubi in *al-Tadhkira* (1:335), Ibn Hajar *(asmâ'ihim* instead of *sîmâhum)* in *Fath al-Bari* (1959 ed. 9:99), and al-Mubarakfuri *(asmâ'ihim* instead of *sîmâhum)* in *Tuhfa al-Ahwadhi* (8:300).

*malakan a'tâhu asmâ'a al-khalâ'iqi fa huwa qâ'imun
'alâ qabrî idhâ mittu falaysa ahadun yusallî 'alayya
salâtan illâ qâla yâ Muhammadu sallâ 'alayka fulânu
ibnu fulânin. Qâla fa yusallî al-Rabbu 'alâ dhâlika al-
rajuli bi kulli wâhidatin 'ashrâ.)* [72]

---

[72]Narrated from 'Ammar ibn Yâsir by Abu al-Shaykh in *al-'Azama*
(1988 ed. 2:763) and al-Bazzar in his *Musnad* (Ibn Hajar, *Mukhtasar*
2:436 #2164), and from Abu Bakr al-Siddiq by al-Daylami in al-
Suyuti's *al-La'ali' al-Masnu'a* (1996 ed. 1:260 =1981 ed. 1:284) and
al-Haba'ik fî Akhbar al-Mala'ik (p. 99).
   Al-Haythami in *Majma' al-Zawa'id* (10:162) said: "Its chains
contain Nu'aym ibn Damdam whom some scholars declared weak and
'Imran ibn al-Himyari [al-Ju'fi], whom al-Bukhari indicated was
unconfirmable *(lâ yutâba')* [i.e. very weak], while the author of *Mizan
al-I'tidal* [al-Dhahabi] declared him unknown. The rest of its sub-
narrators are the men of the *Sahih*." There are some inaccuracies in this
report. Al-Bukhari actually stated in *al-Tarikh al-Kabir* (6:416 #2831):
"He is unconfirmable in his narration of that hadith" as cited by Ibn
'Adi in *al-Kamil* (5:93 #1273). Al-Dhahabi in the *Mizan* (3:236 #6278)
did not declare Ibn al-Himyari unknown, but said: "His narration of the
hadith 'Allah has given me an angel' is not known, and al-Bukhari
said: he is unconfirmable in narrating it.'" Ibn Hajar names him 'Imran
ibn Himyar and similarly states in *Lisan al-Mizan* (4:345 #996): "His
narration of 'Allah has given me an angel' is not known." However,
Ibn Hibban includes him in the *Thiqat* (5:223 #4608) and Ibn Abi
Hatim mentions him without discrediting him in *al-Jarh wa al-Ta'dil*
(6:296 #1644). As for Nu'aym ibn Damdam, Ibn Hajar in *Lisan al-
Mizan* (6:169 #595) stated: "From him narrated Sufyan ibn 'Uyayna,
Abu Ahmad al-Zubayri, Qubaysa ibn 'Uqba, 'Abd al-Rahman ibn Salih
al-Kufi, and others... and I was so far unable to discover who had
declared him weak." Accordingly the chain of the hadith is fair because
Nu'aym's unknown state is eliminated and his credibility is established
by the fact that two or more trutworthy authorities narrated from him,
according to the rules of hadith science. Lastly, al-Daylami's chain
contains neither Nu'aym nor 'Imran.
   Al-'Uqayli cited the narration in his *Du'afa'* (3:248 #1246) and
said: "''Ali ibn al-Qasim al-Kindi from Nu'aym ibn Damdam is a Shi'i
chain of transmission that needs investigation." Al-Suyuti cited it in
La'ali' al-Masnu'a (1996 ed. 1:259-260 =1981 ed. 1:284) and went on

3a. Also among these hadiths is the narration of Abu al-Darda' already mentioned [**#3**]. Shaykh Ibn Taymiyya said: "This hadith is authentic according to the criterion of Muslim."

2a. Also, the hadith of Abu Hurayra already mentioned [**#2**].

Also, the hadith of Abu Hurayra from the Prophet 襁: "Whoever invokes blessings upon me at my grave I hear him, and whoever invokes blessings on me from afar, I am informed about it." *(Man sallâ*

---

to narrate corroborative proofs for the authenticity of the hadith, among them Ibn Abi Shayba's two *mursal* narrations from the weak *Tâbi'î* Yazid ibn Aban al-Raqashi in his *Musannaf* (2:253, 6:326): "An angel is in charge of all that invoke blessings upon the Prophet 襁 to inform him of it saying: 'So-and-so from your Community has invoked blessings on you.'" Isma'il al-Qadi also narrates it from Yazid in *Fadl al-Salat* (p. 37-38 #27) but with the addition: "on the day of *Jum'a*, and with the wording: "So-and-so from your Community *is invoking* blessings on you."

Al-Suyuti cites 'Ammar's narration in his commentary on al-Nasa'i's *Sunan* (4:110). Al-Mundhiri cites the narration in *al-Targhib* (1994 ed. 2:388) after al-Bazzar, Abu al-Shaykh, and al-Tirmidhi in [*al-'Ilal?*] "*al-Kabir*." The hadith is further confirmed by the sound narrations already mentioned and those that follow, as well as the *Tâbi'î* Ayyub al-Sikhtyani's sound *mursal* narration in Isma'il al-Qadi's *Fadl al-Salat* (p. 36): "It has reached me – and Allah knows best – that there is an angel in charge of each person that invokes blessings on the Prophet 襁 so that he will convey it to him." Al-Tabari in the commentary on the verse ❰**For him are angels ranged before him and behind him who guard him by Allah's command**❱ (13:11) in his *Tafsir* (13:115) narrates from 'Uthman ibn 'Affan that the Prophet 襁 identified the angels that attend every believer as twenty, ten in the day and ten in the night, among them two angels whose unique responsibility is to record one's invocations of blessings upon the Prophet 襁. See also al-Albani, *Silsila Sahiha* (#1530).

*'alayya 'inda qabrî sami'tuhu wa man sallâ nâ'iyan
bullightuhu.)* [73] The narrations to that effect are very
numerous indeed.

---

[73] A sound (?) hadith narrated from Abu Hurayra, not by Ibn Abi
Shayba but:

- By al-Bayhaqi with two chains – with *ublightuhu* in the end – in
  Shu'ab al-Iman (2:218 #1583). One chain is very weak because of
  Muhammad ibn Marwan al-Suddi who is accused of lying, and the
  other is weak because of al-'Ala' ibn 'Amr al-Kufi, but al-Bayhaqi
  in *Hayat al-Anbiya'* cites corroborating chains and narrations
  which strengthen the hadith.

- By Abu al-Shaykh – with a third chain – in *al-Salat 'ala al-Nabi*
  🌺 as stated by Ibn al-Qayyim in *Jala' al-Afham* (p. 48-49=p. 16-
  22) and by Ibn Hajar in *Fath al-Bari* (1989 ed. 6:379=1959 ed.
  6:488). Ibn al-Qayyim states: "This narration is extremely strange"
  while Ibn Hajar states: "Abu al-Shaykh cites it in *al-Thawab* with
  a good chain *(sanad jayyid)*." Al-Sakhawi reiterates the latter
  verdict in *al-Qawl al-Badi'* (p. 154) as reported by Shaykh 'Abd
  Allah Siraj al-Din in *al-Salat 'ala al-Nabi* 🌺 (p. 214). Al-Munawi
  questions this grading in *Fayd al-Qadir* and Ibn 'Abd al-Hadi in
  al-Sarim al-Munki (p. 206) avers that Abu al-Shaykh's chain,
  although strong, is "a gross mistake" because the hadith did not
  come to us except through al-Suddi, who is discarded. However,
  Ibn 'Arraq in *Tanzih al-Shari'a* (1:335) confirms Ibn Hajar's
  verdict and al-Suyuti in *al-La'ali' al-Masnu'a* (1996 ed. 1:259 =
  1:282-283) adduces Abu al-Shaykh's chain – among other
  narrations – as corroboration for the hadith, citing it in his
  commentary on al-Nasa'i's *Sunan* (4:110) and rejecting Ibn al-
  Jawzi's verdict of forgery in *al-Mawdu'at* (1:303).

- By al-Khatib in *Tarikh Baghdad* (3:292) with the very weak chain
  of Muhammad ibn Marwan al-Suddi with the wording: "Whoever
  invokes blessings upon me at my grave I hear him, and whoever
  invokes blessings on me from afar, an angel was put in charge of it
  who informs me of it. He will have sufficiency of his worldly
  needs for it as well as his needs in the hereafter, and I shall witness
  on his behalf – or: I shall be his intercessor." Al-Ahdab in his
  Zawa'id Tarikh Baghdad (3:69) considers the second sentence of
  this narration undoubtedly forged.

IV.   The Prophet ﷺ Answers Whoever Calls Him

The Prophet ﷺ answers whoever calls him with the words: "O Muhammad!" as stated in the hadith of Abu Hurayra in Abu Ya'la's *Musnad*:

> 21. The Prophet ﷺ said: "By the one in Whose hand is Abu al-Qasim's soul, 'Isa ibn Maryam shall descend as a just and wise ruler. He shall destroy the cross, slay the swine, eradicate discord and grudges, and money shall be offered to him but he will not accept it. Then he shall stand at my grave side and say: 'O Muhammad!' and I will answer him."[74]

The hadith master Ibn Hajar cites it in *al-Matalib al-'Aliya*, in the chapter entitled: "Concerning the Prophet's ﷺ life in his grave."[75]

V.   The Sending of *Salâm* by Courier to the Prophet ﷺ

> 22. Yazid al-Mahdi narrates: "When I bade farewell [from *Shâm*] to 'Umar ibn 'Abd al-'Aziz ﷺ he said to me: 'I have a service to ask of you.' I said: 'O Commander of the Believers! What service do you need of me?' He said: 'I need of you, when you arrive at Madina and see the grave of the Prophet ﷺ, to

---

[74]Narrated from Abu Hurayra by Abu Ya'la in his *Musnad* (11:462) with a sound *(sahîh)* chain according to Shaykh Husayn Asad and al-Haythami in *Majma' al-Zawa'id* (8:211).
[75]Ibn Hajar, *al-Matalib al-'Aliya* (4:23 and #4574).

pronounce *salâm* to him on my behalf.'" Similarly,
Hatim ibn Wardân narrates: "'Umar ibn 'Abd al-'Aziz
⁣ used to send his courier from *Shâm* with the
message to convey his greetings to Allah's
Messenger."[76]

Al-Qadi 'Iyad narrated it in *al-Shifa'*, in the chapter on
visiting the Prophet ﷺ. Al-Khafaji and Mulla 'Ali al-Qari
mentioned in their commentaries that Ibn Abi al-Dunya and al-
Bayhaqi had narrated it in the *Shu'ab*. Al-Fayruzabadi
mentioned it in *al-Silat wa al-Bushr*.[77] Al-Khafaji said: "It was
the habit of the *Salaf* to send their greetings to the Prophet ﷺ.
Ibn 'Umar used to send his greetings to him ﷺ, to Abu Bakr ⁣,
and to 'Umar ⁣. Even if our greetings to the Prophet ﷺ reach
him from afar, nevertheless, there is a special merit in addressing
him at his grave and receiving the greeting in return from him."[78]

---

[76]Narrated by al-Qadi 'Iyad in *al-Shifa'* al-Bayhaqi in *Shu'ab al-Iman*
(#4166), al-Samhudi, *Wafa' al-Wafa'* (p. 1357), Ibn Jama'a in *Hidaya
al-Salik* (3:1381), Ibn al-Jawzi in *Muthir al-Gharam* (p. 486-498), and
others.

[77]Al-Fayruzabadi, *al-Silat wa al-Bushr* (p. 153).

[78]Al-Khafaji, *Nasim al-Riyad* (2:516). Al-Sakhawi said in *al-Qawl al-
Badi'* (p. 159-160): "Shaykh al-Islam (Taqi al-Din) al-Subki said in his
book *Shifa' al-Siqam*: 'A large number of imams have inferred from
the hadith "No one greets me except Allah has returned my soul to me
so that I can return his salam" [see #2 above] the desirability *(istihbâb)*
of visiting the grave of the Prophet ﷺ.' I say: This is a sound inference
because when the visitor greets the Prophet ﷺ his reply is given from
near, and this is a benefit much sought-after which Allah has made
easily available for us to return again and again to the very beginning
of that blessing."

Shaykh Muhammad ibn 'Alawi also said in his *Mafahim Yajib
an Tusahhah*: "Some people – may Allah reform them and guide them
to the straight path – look at the grave of our Most Honored Prophet ﷺ
from the mere perspective that it is a grave like any other. It is no
wonder that all sorts of wrong imaginings and bad thoughts occur in
their minds and hearts with regard to the Muslims who do visit the

Prophet ﷺ and travel for that purpose and stand at his grave making *du'â*. Such people may be heard objecting: 'It is forbidden to travel to his grave,' and 'it is forbidden to make *du'â* at his grave.' Indeed they will push their denial to the point that they say: '*Du'â* at his grave constitutes idolatry *(shirk)* or disbelief *(kufr)*,' or 'Whoever says that the grave is the most blessed spot on earth including the Ka'ba, has committed *shirk* and is misguided.' And this wholesale blind and thoughtless condemnation of others with the charges of disbelief and misguidance *(dalâl)* contravenes the way of the pious *Salaf*. No two people can be found who will not agree on what is meant when we speak of the Noble Grave or the visit to it or its preference or travelling to it or invoking Allah and asking Him in front of the grave. There is no qualm nor divergence about the meaning of all this among Muslims. Clearly, the meaning of what is sought after is the inhabitant of the grave himself: the Master of all Prophets and the best of all of Allah's creations, the greatest Prophet and the most noble Messenger, blessings and peace upon him and upon his Family."

There is Consensus among the scholars of *Ahl al-Sunna* that the Prophet's ﷺ grave is the most blessed spot on earth including the Ka'ba according to al-Qadi 'Iyad in *al-Shifa'*, al-Qari in *Sharh al-Shifa'* (Dar al-Kutub al-'Ilmiyya 2:162), al-Nawawi in *Sharh Sahih Muslim* (al-Mays ed. 9/10:172-173) and *al-Majmu' Sharh al-Muhadhdhab* (7:444), Ibn 'Aqil al-Hanbali as quoted by Ibn al-Qayyim in *Bada'i' al-Fawa'id*, Ibn 'Abidin in his *Hashiya*, and others. In their century-old *fatwa* on visitation to the Prophet ﷺ the scholars of Deoband and other parts of India stated: "That noble spot and enlightened expanse of space which contains his limbs – blessings and peace upon him – is absolutely more meritorious even than the Ka'ba, the Throne, and the *kursî*, as explicitly declared by our *fuqahâ'*.... The sun of the pious scholars, our shaykh, Mawlana Rashid Ahmad al-Gangohi has expounded upon this matter in the same terms that we used, or even more explicitly, in his treatise *Zubda al-Manasik fi Fadl Ziyara al-Madina al-Munawwara*, which has been printed several times. Also relevant to this noble issue is the treatise of the shaykh of our shaykhs, Mawlana Sadr al-Din al-Dihlawi – may Allah sanctify his precious secret – in his treatise *Ahsan al-Maqal fi Hadith la Tushadd al-Rihal* which came out in print and became well-known, and in which he unleashed disaster on the heads of those who call themselves '*salafiyya*.'" In Muhammad ibn 'Alawi, *Shifa' al-Fu'ad* (p. 83-88).

VI. *Salâm* and *Adhân* Heard From the Noble Grave

The Imam and hadith master Abu Muhammad 'Abd Allah al-Darimi narrated in his book *al-Sunan* which is numbered among the Six fundamental books of hadith:[79]

23. Marwan ibn Muhammad told us: From Sa'id ibn 'Abd al-'Aziz who said: "During the events of al-Harra [80] there was no *adhân* in the Prophet's 🌸 mosque for three days, nor *iqâma*. At that time Sa'id ibn al-Musayyib did not leave the mosque at all. He would not know the time of prayer except from a humming sound that he would hear coming from the Prophet's 🌸 grave.[81]

---

[79]"Some scholars count al-Darimi's *Sunan* among the Six Books instead of Ibn Majah's *Sunan*." Abu Ghudda in al-Lucknawi's *Tuhfa al-Akhyar* (p. 64 n.). Shah Wali Allah and others also count Imam Malik's *Muwatta'* among the Six Books. See Shaykh Muhammad ibn 'Alawi's *al-Manhal al-Latif fi 'Ulum al-Hadith*.

[80]*Al-Harra* is the name of a place near Madina and refers to the sacking of Madina by the armies of *Shâm* under Yazid ibn Mu'awiya in the year 63, at which time al-Zuhri stated that ten thousand of the people of Madina were killed, among them seven hundred of the *Muhâjirûn* and *Ansâr* as related by Ibn Kathir in *al-Bidaya wa al-Nihaya* (Maktaba al-Ma'arif ed. 8:221).

[81]Narrated with a sound chain from Sa'id ibn 'Abd al-'Aziz al-Tannukhi by al-Darimi in his *Sunan*, from Abu Hazim Salama ibn Dinar and Muhammad ibn Sa'id ibn al-Musayyib by Ibn Sa'd in *al-Tabaqat al-Kubra* (5:132) and al-Dhahabi in the *Siyar* (Arna'ut ed. 4:228-229), also by Ibn al-Jawzi in *Muthir al-Gharam* (p. 486-498) and al-Suyuti in *al-Khasa'is al-Kubra* (2:490). Some of the above sources add the following version: Abu Hazim said: I heard Sa'id ibn al-Musayyib say: "During the nights of al-Harra there were no people in the Prophet's 🌸 mosque except myself. The people of *Shâm* would enter in groups and say: 'Look at that crazy old man!' and whenever

Shaykh Muhammad ibn 'Abd al-Wahhab related this report in his *Ahkam Tamanni al-Mawt* which was published among his collected works.[82]

24. Imam Majd al-Din al-Fayruzabadi related the following report: Ibrahim ibn Shayban said: "One year I went on pilgrimage then I came to Madina and approached the grave of the Prophet 鑾 and said *Salâm* to him. I heard, coming from inside the room, the reply: "*Wa 'alayka al-salâm.*"[83]

---

the time of prayer came, I would hear *adhân* coming from the Prophet's 鑾 grave. I would step forward, call *iqâma* and pray, and there would be no one in the mosque but me."

[82]Muhammad ibn 'Abd al-Wahhab, *Majmu'a al-Mu'allafat* (3:47).

[83]Narrated from Muhammed ibn Hibban by Abu Nu'aym, *al-Targhib* (#102), Ibn al-Najjar, *Akhbar al-Madina* (p. 146), Ibn al-Jawzi in *Muthir al-Gharam* (p. 486-498), al-Fayruzabadi in *al-Silat wa al-Bushr* (p. 54), and Ibn Taymiyya in *Iqtida' al-Sirat al-Mustaqim* (p. 373-374).

II.
The Prophet's 鄒 *Isrâ'* and *Mi'râj* [84]

I. Introduction

Praise be to Allah Who has chosen His praiseworthy servant Muhammad 鄒 for the Message, distinguished him with the night journey on the lightning-mount Burâq, and caused him to ascend on the ladders of perfection to the high heavens to show him of the greatest signs of his Lord. He raised him until he reached to the Lote-tree of the Farthest Boundary where ends the science of every Messenger-Prophet and every Angel Brought Near, where lies the Garden of Retreat, to the point that he heard the sound of the pens that write what befell and what is to befall.

There He manifested Himself to him through vision and addressed him intimately in the station of encounter, accompanying him so that he was no longer alone. There He stilled his fear in those lofty worlds and communicated to him what He wished, revealed to him what He wished, taught him what He wished, and explained to him what He wished. He showed him some of the signs of sovereignty and the signs of creation and the unseen that point to the uniqueness and perfection of His immense majesty, the marvels of His lordly power, and the sublimity of His wisdom without beginning. Glory to Him, the God that knows the heart's secret and its confidence, and knows what is more subtle and more hidden! He hears the patter of the black ant's feet on a massive rock in the dark night.

---

[84]From Shaykh Muhammad ibn 'Alawi's book *al-Anwar al-Bahiyya min Isra' wa Mi'raj Khayr al-Bariyya* (Mecca: s.n., 1414/1993).

I bear witness that there is no God but Allah, Who is sanctified in His essence from all figurative representation and shades, and elevated above having a partner in His attributes and acts. I bear witness that our master Muhammad is His servant and Messenger 🕌, whose rank He has raised so that none of the seven skies can reach it, nor any of the Prophets. For how could they reach his stature when they were shown to him in the Sanctified House in Jerusalem where Gibrîl 🕌 gave him precedence over them so that he led them in prayer, then apprised him of their places and stations in the heavens, thereby showing that he is their paramount chief and foremost leader since the beginning?

Allah bore witness that the Prophet 🕌 was the Guide through his knowledge and the Just Instructor in his actions. He elevated his speaking manner above vanity and disgrace; He freed his innermost being from belying what his eyes saw; and He warded his eyes from falsehood and transgression. Then he saw his Lord, in the station of Proximity and Servanthood. Nor did he fall short of uncovering the reality of the event, but he received all that was communicated to him of both partial and total knowledge.

May Allah's blessing and peace be upon him and upon his Family, the People of Guidance and Firmness, and upon his excellent and pure Companions, carriers of the trusts of Prophetic Inheritance, defenders of the precious Religion with every burnished sword, who have triumphed and won the highest dwellings in the Abode of Eternity.

To begin, the indigent in need of the mercy of his generous Lord, Muhammad ibn 'Alawi ibn 'Abbas al-Maliki al-Hasani says – may Allah treat him with His radiant kindness: Allah has granted me the favor of writing a vast treatise covering the substantial research which has been done on the subject of *al-isrâ' wa al-mi'râj.* Then He expanded my breast so that I could gather its account into a single text as a separate monograph so as to allow its access to the people at large. In this way they can familiarize themselves with that text and recite it in the public meetings and great celebrations in which Muslims gather to commemorate *al-isrâ' wa al-mi'râj,* as is the custom in many countries, especially in the two Holy Sanctuaries.

I have collated my own work with that of the hadith master al-Shami[85] and Najm al-Din al-Ghayti[86] to make a single comprehensive text with the mention of additions in their appropriate places. This text includes most of the different narrations on this subject. I have provided a concise commentary and brief notes explaining the meaning of rare or difficult words. I have named this treatise: *al-Anwar al-Bahiyya Min Isra' wa Mi'raj Khayr al-Bariyya,* "The Resplendent Lights of the Night-Journey and Ascension of the Best of Creation," asking Allah to grant much benefit through it and accept it as purely for His

---

[85] *Al-Ayât al-'Azima al-Bahira fi Mi'raj Sayyid Ahl al-Dunya wa al-Akhira* in 17 chapters by the hadith master Shams al-Din Muhammad ibn Yusuf ibn 'Ali al-Shami al-Dimashqi al-Salihi Nazil al-Qahira (d. 942), al-Suyuti's student, author of a ten-volume biography of the Prophet entitled *Subul al-Huda wa al-Rashad fi Sira Khayr al-'Ibad* which he compiled from over three hundred sources and which his student Muhammad ibn Muhammad ibn Ahmad al-Fishi al-Maliki edited and published. He also authored *'Uqud al-Juman fi Manaqib Abi Hanifa al-Nu'man, al-Fawa'id al-Majmu'a fi Bayan al-Ahadith al-Mawdu'a* [a title also used by al-Shawkani], *al-Ithaf bi Tamyiz Ma Tabi'a fihi al-Baydawi Sahib al-Kashshaf,* and others. See al-Kattani, *al-Risala al-Mustatrafa* (p. 151, 199-200).

[86] *Al-Ibtihaj fi al-Kalam 'ala al-Isra' wa al-Miraj* by the hadith scholar Najm al-Din Abu al-Mawahib Muhammad ibn Ahmad ibn 'Ali ibn Abi Bakr al-Ghayti al-Sakandari al-Masri al-Shafi'i (d. 981). See al-Kattani, *al-Risala al-Mustatrafa* (p. 200). Al-Ghayti's work was published under the title *Mawsu'a al-Isra' wa al-Mi'raj al-Musamma Tatriz al-Dibaj bi Haqa'iq al-Isra' wa al-Mi'raj* (Beirut: Dar wa-Maktaba al-Hilal, 1994).

sake. Allah's blessings and peace be upon our master
Muhammad and his Family and Companions!

II.   The Striving of the Scholars to Organize the Account of *Isrâ'* and *Mi'râj* Into A Single Version

The scholars have striven to organize this account and
gather its narrations into a single narrative, at the same time
making mention of a few variant additions, in order to facilitate
its perusal and benefit. In this way they gathered the narrations
in one place for the people at large. This is permitted according
to the rules of the experts in the field of hadith as stated by them.
Many of them have used this method in many instances in which
they would join up together the several narrations of different
narrators of a single event as was done with the Farewell
Pilgrimage and some of the military raids and campaigns. The
hadith master al-Shami did this with the account of the Prophet's
Night-Journey and Ascension as well as the hadith master al-
Ghayti and a number of other scholars. Of use here is what al-
Shami said on this question in his great book al-*Mi'raj*:

> Know – may Allah have mercy on me and you! –
> that each of the hadiths of the Companions [on this
> subject] contains what the other does not.[87] Therefore I
> consulted Allah Almighty and concatenated them,
> rearranging the account into a single narrative so that it

---

[87]Al-Kattani in *Nazm al-Mutanathir in al-hadith al-Mutawatir* (p. 207-
209) listed as forty-five the number of the Companions who related
something pertaining to the Prophet's 鬱 night-journey. Accordingly,
the scholars have graded the event of *isrâ'* as mass-transmitted
(mutawâtir), together with the facts that it took place on top of the
Burâq and that the Prophet Idris 鬱 is in the Fourth Heaven.

would be sweeter to attentive ears, and in order for its benefit to suit all occasions.

If someone says: "Each hadith of the *mi'râj* differs from the next and the ascensions may number according to the number of their accounts: why then did you make all of them into a single account?" I say: The author of *Zad al-Ma'ad* [Ibn al-Qayyim] said:

> This is the path of the feeble-minded among the literalists of the *Zahirî* school who are authorities in transmitted texts. If they see in the account a wording that differs from the version of one of the narrators they multiply the occurrence of the event accordingly. The correct view is what the Imams of text transmission have said: namely, that the *mi'râj* took place once, in Mecca, after the beginning of Prophethood. It is a wonder how these have claimed that it took place repeatedly. How can they countenance the conclusion that every time, fifty prayers are prescribed upon him then he goes back and forth between Musa and his Lord until they become five, and his Lord says: "I have decreed what is due Me and have reduced the burden of My slaves," only for him to come a second time with fifty prayers which he decreases again, ten by ten?[88]

The hadith master 'Imad al-Din Ibn Kathir said in his history, after noting that Malik ibn Sa'sa'a's version did not make mention of al-Quds:

> Some of the narrators would omit part of the report due to its being known, or due to forgetfulness, or because he would mention only what he considered important, or

---

[88]Ibn al-Qayyim, *Zad al-Ma'ad* (3:38).

because one time he would feel eager to relate it completely, while another time he would tell his public what is of most use to them.

He who relates every differing narration to a separate occurrence thereby affirming several ascensions has strayed widely and said something indefensible, failing to fulfill his pursuit. The reason is that all of the versions contain his meeting with the Prophets and the prescription of the prayers upon him: how then could one defend multiplying these occurrences? This understanding is extremely far-fetched nor was it related from any of the Salaf, whereas if this had indeed taken place several times the Prophet would have reported it to his Community and the people would have transmitted it often.[89]

---

[89]Ibn Kathir, *al-Bidaya wa al-Nihaya* (al-Ma'arif ed. 3:117).

III.   The Collated Hadith of *Isrâ'* and *Mi'râj*

Allah's Blessings and Peace
upon the Messenger of Allah
and his Family and Companions

As the Prophet 鹏 was in al-Hijr at the House,[90] lying down at rest between two men,[91] Gibrîl and Mîkâ'îl came to him. With them was a third angel.[92] They carried him until they brought him to the spring of Zamzam, where they asked him to lie on his back and Gibrîl took him over from the other two. (Another version says:) "The roof of my house was opened and Gibrîl descended."

He split the Prophet's 鹏 chest from his throat to the bottom of his belly. Then Gibrîl said to Mîkâ'îl: "Bring me a *tast*[93] of water from Zamzam so that I will purify his heart and expand his breast." He took out his heart and washed it three times, removing from it what was wrong. Mîkâ'îl went back and forth to him with the vessel of water from Zamzam three times.

Then he brought him a golden vessel filled with wisdom and belief which he emptied into his chest. He filled his chest

---

[90] Al-Hijr is the semi-circular space under the waterspout which is open on both sides on the Northwest side of the Ka'ba.
[91] His uncle Hamza 鹏 and his cousin Ja'far ibn Abi Talib 鹏.
[92] Isrâfîl.
[93] A vessel, usually made of copper.

with *hilm*,[94] knowledge, certainty, and submission, then he closed it up. He sealed it between his shoulders with the seal of Prophethood.

Then he brought the Burâq, handsome-faced and bridled, a tall, white beast, bigger than the donkey but smaller than the mule. He could place his hooves at the farthest boundary of his gaze. He had long ears. Whenever he faced a mountain his hind legs would extend, and whenever he went downhill his front legs would extend. He had two wings on his thighs which lent strength to his legs.

He bucked when the Prophet 🕌 came to mount him. Gibrîl put his hand on his mane and said: "Are you not ashamed, O Burâq? By Allah, none has mounted you in all creation dearer to Allah than he." Hearing this he was so ashamed that he sweated until he became soaked, and he stood still so that the Prophet 🕌 mounted him.

The other Prophets used to mount the Burâq before. Sa'id ibn al-Musayyib said: "It is the beast of Ibrahim which he used to mount whenever he travelled to the Sacred House."

Gibrîl departed with him. He placed himself on his right while Mîkâ'îl was on his left. (In Ibn Sa'd's version:) The one holding his stirrup was Gibrîl and the one holding the reins of the Burâq was Mîkâ'îl.

They travelled until they reached a land filled with datepalms. Gibrîl said to the Prophet 🕌: "Alight and pray here." He did so and remounted, then Gibrîl said: "Do you know where you prayed?" He said no. Gibrîl said: "You prayed in a *tayba* or land of pastures, and the Migration will take place there.

---

[94] *Hilm* denotes intelligence, patience, gentleness, and good character.

The Burâq continued his lightning flight, placing his hooves wherever his gaze could reach. Gibrîl then said again: "Alight and pray here." He did so and remounted, then Gibrîl said: "Do you know where you prayed?" He said no. Gibrîl said: "You prayed in Madyan[95] at the tree of Musa."[96]

The Burâq continued his lightning flight, then Gibrîl said again: "Alight and pray here." He did so and remounted, then Gibrîl said: "Do you know where you prayed?" He said no. Gibrîl said: "You prayed at the mountain of Sînâ' where Allah addressed Musa."[97]

Then he reached a land where the palaces of *al-Shâm* became visible to him. Gibrîl said to him: "Alight and pray." He did so and remounted, then the Burâq continued his lightning flight and Gibrîl said: "Do you know where you prayed?" He said no. Gibrîl said: "You prayed in Bayt Lahm, where 'Isa ibn Maryam was born."[98]

As the Prophet 鑾 was travelling mounted on the Burâq he saw a devil from the jinn who was trying to get near him holding a firebrand. Everywhere the Prophet 鑾 turned he would see him. Gibrîl said to him: "Shall I teach you words which, if you say them, his firebrand will go out and he will fall dead?" The Prophet 鑾 said yes. Gibrîl said:

> Say: *a'ûdhu bi wajhillâhi al-karîm*
> *wa bi kalimâtillâhi al-tâmmât*

---

[95] A city on the shore of the Red Sea bordering Tabuk near the valley of Shu'ayb.
[96] The tree under which Musa 鑾 rested from fatigue and hunger during his flight from Fir'awn
[97] Mount Sinai.
[98] Bethlehem.

al-lâtî la yujâwizuhunna bârrun wa la fâjir
min sharri ma yanzilu min al-samâ'
wa min sharri ma ya'ruju fîhâ
wa min sharri ma dhara'a fi al-ard
wa min sharri ma yakhruju minhâ
wa min fitani al-layli wa al-nahâr
wa min tawâriq al-layli wa al-nahâr
illa târiqin yatruqu bi khayrin ya rahmân

I seek refuge in Allah's Blessed Face
and in Allah's perfect words
which neither the righteous nor the disobedient overstep
from evil that descends from the heaven
and evil that ascends to it
and evil that is created in the earth
and the trials of night and day
and the visitors of night and day
save the visitor that visits goodness upon us,
O Beneficent One!

At this the devil fell dead on his face and his firebrand went out.

They travelled until they reached a people who sowed in a day and reaped in a day. Every time they reaped, their harvest would be replenished as before. The Prophet 🕮 said: "O Gibrîl! What is this?" He replied: "These are *al-mujâhidûn*, those who strive in the path of Allah the Exalted. Every good deed of theirs is multiplied for them seven hundred times, and whatever they spend returns multiplied."

The Prophet 🕮 then noticed a fragrant wind and said: "O Gibrîl, what is this sweet scent?" He replied:

This is the scent of the lady who combed the hair of Fir'awn's[99] daughter and that of her children. As she combed the hair of Fir'awn's daughter the comb fell and she said: "*Bismillâh ta'isa Fir'awn* – In the name of Allah, perish Fir'awn!" whereupon Fir'awn's daughter said: "Do you have a Lord other than my father?" She said yes. Fir'awn's daughter said: "Shall I tell my father?" She said yes. She told him and he summoned her and said: "Do you have a Lord other than me?" She replied: "Yes, my Lord and your Lord is Allah."

This woman had two sons and a husband. Fir'awn summoned them and he began to entice the woman and her husband to give up their religion, but they refused. He said: "Then I shall have you killed." She said: "Please bury us all together in a single grave if you kill us." He replied: "Granted, and it is your right to ask us." He then ordered that a huge cow made of copper be filled with boiling liquid[100] and that she and her children be thrown into it. The children were taken and thrown in one after the other. The second and youngest was still an infant at the breast. When they took him he said: "Mother! fall and do not tarry for verily you are on the right." Then she was thrown in with her children.

Ibn 'Abbas said: "Four spoke from the cradle as they were still infants: this child, Yusuf's witness,[101] Jurayj's companion, and 'Isa ibn Maryam."[102]

---

[99]Pharaoh.
[100]Oil and water.
[101] (12:26).
[102]Narrated by Bukhari and Muslim. Ibn Hajar mentions that the account of the lady who combed the hair of Pharaoh's daughter is narrated from Ibn 'Abbas by Ahmad, al-Hakim, Ibn Hibban, and al-

Then the Prophet 🕌 saw some people whose heads were being shattered, then every time they would return to their original state and be shattered again without delay. He said: "O Gibrîl, who are these people?" He replied: "These are the people whose heads were too heavy [on their pillows] to get up and fulfill the prescribed prayers."

Then he saw a people who wore loincloths on the fronts and on their backs. They were roaming the way camels and sheep roam about. They were eating thistles and *zaqqûm* – the fruit of a tree that grows in hell and whose fruit resembles the head of devils[103] – and white-hot coals and stones of Hell-Fire. He said: "Who are these, O Gibrîl?" He replied: "These are the ones who did not meet the obligation of paying alms from what they possessed, while Allah never withheld anything from them."

Then he saw a people who had in front of them excellent meats disposed in pots and also putrid meat, and they would eat

---

Bazzar. Muslim in his *Sahih*, Book of *al-zuhd wa al-raqa'iq* (#3005) mentions the part of the infant speaking to his mother before they are both thrown into the fire. The mention of Yusuf's witness in the verse ❨And a witness, one of her own folk, testified❩ (12:26) as being an infant is narrated from Ibn 'Abbas by Ibn Abi Hatim with a weak chain, but is retained by al-Hasan al-Basri and Sa'id ibn Jubayr. It is also the explanation retained by al-Suyuti and others in their commentaries of the Qur'an. This brings the number of speaking infants alluded to in the hadith "Those who spoke from the cradle are three" (Bukhari, Muslim, Ahmad) up to five, and there are reports that increase it to seven or more. Allah knows best. *Fath al-Bari* (1989 ed. 6:593-594).

[103] ❨Is this better as a welcome, or the tree of Zaqqûm? Lo! We have appointed it a torment for wrong doers. Lo! it is a tree that springs in the heart of hell. Its crop is as it were the heads of devils. And lo! they verily must eat thereof, and fill (their) bellies therewith❩ (37:62-66).

from the foul meat and not touch the good meat. He said: "What is this, O Gibrîl?" He replied: "These are the men from your Community who had an excellent, lawful wife at home and who would go and see an infamous woman and spend the night with her; and the women who would leave her excellent, lawful husband to go and see a infamous man and spend the night with him."

Then he came to a plank in the middle of the road which not even a piece of cloth nor less than that could cross except it would be pierced. He said: "What is this, O Gibrîl?" He replied: "This is what happens to those of your Community who sit in the middle of the road and harm passers-by" and he recited: **❨Lurk not on every road to threaten wayfarers and to turn away from Allah's path him who believes in Him, and to seek to make it crooked❩** (7:86).[104]

The Prophet saw a man swimming in a river of blood and he was being struck in his mouth with rocks which he then swallowed. The Prophet asked: "What is this, O Gibrîl?" He replied: "This is what happens to those who eat usury."

Then he saw a man who had gathered a stack of wood which he could not carry, yet he was adding more wood to it. He said: "What is this, O Gibrîl?" He replied: "This is a man from your Community who gets people's trusts when he cannot fulfill them, yet he insists on carrying them.

He then saw people whose tongues and lips were being sliced with metal knives. Every time they were sliced they would return to their original state to be sliced again without respite. He said: "Who are these, O Gibrîl?" He replied: "These are the

---

[104]See n. 127.

public speakers of division in your Community: they say what they don't do."

Then he passed by people who had copper nails with which they scratched their own faces and chests. He asked: "Who are these, O Gibrîl?" He replied: "These are the ones who ate the flesh of people and tarnished their reputations."

Then he saw a small hole with a huge bull coming out of it. The bull began to try entering the hole again and was unable. The Prophet 🕮 said: "What is this, O Gibrîl?" He replied: "This is the one in your Community who tells an enormity, then he feels remorse to have spoken it but is unable to take it back."

(Al-Shami added:) He then came to a valley in which he breathed a sweet, cool breeze fragrant with musk and he heard a voice. He said: "What is this, O Gibrîl?" He replied: "This is the voice of Paradise saying:

O my Lord, bring me what You have promised me!
Too abundant are my rooms, my gold-laced garments,
My silk, my brocades, my carpets, my pearls, my corals,
My silver, my gold, my goblets, my bowls, my pitchers,
My couches, my honey, my water, my milk, my wine!

And the Lord says:

You shall have every single Muslim man and woman,
Every believing man and woman,
Everyone who has believed in Me and My Messengers
And did excellent deeds
Without associating a partner with Me
Nor taking helpers without Me!
Anyone who fears Me shall be safe,
And whoever asks of Me, I shall give him,

And whoever loans Me something, I shall repay him,
And whoever relies upon Me, I shall suffice him!
I am Allâh *besides Whom there is no God.*
I never fail in My promise.
〈Successful indeed are the believers.〉 (23:1)
〈So blessed be Allah, the best of Creators!〉 (23:14)

And Paradise answers: I accept."

Then the Prophet 🕌 came to a valley in which he heard
a detestable sound and smelled a foul wind. He said: "What is
this, O Gibrîl?" He replied: "This is the sound of Hell-Fire saying:

O Lord, give me what You promised me!
Abundant are my chains, my yokes, my punishments,
My fires, my thistles, my pus, my tortures!
My depth is abysmal, my heat unbearable!
Therefore give me what You promised me!

And the Lord replies:

You shall have every idolater and idolatress,
Every disbelieving man and woman, every foul one,
And every tyrant who does not believe
in the Day of Reckoning!"

The Prophet 🕌 saw the Anti-Christ *(al-Dajjâl)* in his
actual likeness. He saw him with his own eyes, not in a dream. It
was said to him: "O Messenger of Allah, how was he when you
saw him?" He replied: "Mammoth-sized *(faylamâniyyan)*, extremely pale and white *(aqmaru hijan)*, and one of his eyes is pro-

tuberant as if it were a twinkling star. His hair is like the branches of a tree. He resembles 'Abd al-'Uzza ibn Qatan."[105]

The Prophet 鑾 saw a pearl-like white column which the angels were carrying. He said: "What is this you are carrying?" They replied: "The Column of Islam. We have been ordered to place it in *al-Shâm*." (End of al-Shami's addition.)[106]

As the Prophet 鑾 was travelling he heard someone calling him from his right: "O Muhammad! Look at me, I want to ask you something!" But the Prophet 鑾 did not respond. Then he said: "Who was this, O Gibrîl?" He replied: "This is the herald of the Jews. If you had answered him your Community would have followed Judaism."

The Prophet 鑾 continued travelling and he heard someone calling him from his left: "O Muhammad! Look at me, I want to ask you something!" But the Prophet 鑾 did not respond. Then he said: "Who was this, O Gibrîl?" He replied: "This is the herald of the Christians. If you had answered him, your Community would have followed Christianity."

The Prophet 鑾 continued travelling and passed by a woman with bare arms, decked with every female ornament Allah had created. She said: "O Muhammad! Look at me, I need to ask you something." But he did not look at her. Then he said: "Who was this, O Gibrîl?" He replied: "This was the world *(al-dunyâ)*. If you had answered her, your Community would have preferred the world to the hereafter."

As the Prophet 鑾 travelled on, he passed by an old man who was some distance away from his path saying: "Come

---

[105]Ibn Qatan died in the time of ignorance.
[106]See Part III.

hither, O Muhammad!" But Gibrîl said: "Nay! Go on, O Muhammad!" The Prophet 🕌 went on and then said: "Who was this, O Gibrîl?" He replied: "This was Allah's enemy, Iblis. He wanted you to incline towards him."

He went on and passed by an old woman on the roadside who said: "O Muhammad! Look at me, I need to ask you something!" But he did not look at her. Then he said: "Who was this, O Gibrîl?" He replied: "The world has as much left to live as the remaining lifetime of this old woman."

(Al-Shami added:) As he went on he was met by some of Allah's creatures who said: "Peace be upon you, O First One! *(Yâ awwal)*. Peace upon you, O Last One! *(Yâ âkhir)*. Peace be upon you, O Gatherer! *(Yâ hâshir)*." Gibrîl said to him: "Return their greeting," and he did. Then he saw them another time and they said the same thing. Then he saw them a third time and again they greeted him. He said: "Who are they, O Gibrîl?" He replied: "Ibrahim, Musa, and 'Isa."

The Prophet 🕌 then passed by Musa 🕌 as he was praying in his grave at a place of red sandhills. He was tall, with long hair and brown complexion, similar to one of the Shanu'a – the [Yemeni] men of pure lineage and manly virtue. He was saying with a loud voice: "You have honored him and preferred him!" Then the Prophet 🕌 greeted him and he returned his greeting. Musa 🕌 said: "Who is this with you, O Gibrîl?" He replied: "This is Ahmad 🕌." He said: "Welcome to the Arabian Prophet who acted perfectly with his Community!" and he made an invocation for blessing on his behalf. Then he said: "Ask ease for you Community."

They continued travelling and the Prophet 🕌 said: "O Gibrîl! Who was this?" He replied: "This was Musa ibn 'Imran." The Prophet 🕌 asked: "Who was he reprimanding?" He said:

"He was reprimanding his Lord." The Prophet 鑾 said: "He reprimands his Lord and raises his voice against his Lord?!" Gibrîl said: "Allah the Exalted well knows Musa's bluntness."

He passed by a large tree whose fruit seemed like a thornless berry (of the kind that gives shade to men and cattle). Under it an old man was resting with his dependents. There were lamps and a great light could be seen. The Prophet 鑾 said: "Who is this, O Gibrîl?" He replied: "Your father Ibrahim." The Prophet 鑾 greeted him and Ibrahim 鑾 returned his greeting and said: "Who is this with you, O Gibrîl?" He replied: "This is your son Ahmad." Ibrahim 鑾 said:

> Welcome to the unlettered Arabian Prophet who has conveyed the message of his Lord and acted with perfect sincerity with his Community!

> O my son, you are going to meet your Lord tonight, and your Community is the last and the weakest of all Communities – therefore, if you are able to have your need fulfilled concerning your Community, or most of it, be sure to do it!

Then he invoked for goodness on his behalf.

They continued travelling until they reached the valley that is in the city – that is: the Hallowed House [Jerusalem] – when lo and behold! Hell-Fire was shown to them like a carpet unfolded. They [the Companions] said: "O Messenger of Allah! What did it look like?" He replied: "Like cinders."

He continued travelling until he reached the city of the Hallowed House and he entered it by its Southern gate. He dismounted the Burâq and tied it at the gate of the mosque, using the ring by which the Prophets tied it before him. One narration states that Gibrîl came to the Rock and placed his fingers in it, piercing it, then he tied the Burâq using the spot he had hollowed out.

The Prophet ﷺ entered the mosque from a gate through which the sun and the moon could be seen when they set. He prayed two cycles of prayer and did not tarry long before a large throng of people had gathered. The Prophet ﷺ recognized all the Prophets, some standing in prayer, some bowing, some prostrating. Then a caller called out to the prayer and the final call to prayer was made. They rose and stood in lines, waiting for the one who would lead them. Gibrîl took the hand of the Prophet ﷺ and brought him forward. He led them in two cycles of prayer.[107]

The following is related from Ka'b: Gibrîl ﷺ raised the call to prayer. The angels descended from the heaven. Allah gathered all the Messengers and Prophets. Then the Prophet ﷺ prayed as the leader of the angels and Messengers. When he left, Gibrîl asked him: "O Muhammad, do you know who prayed behind you?" He said no. Gibrîl said: "Every single Prophet whom Allah has ever sent." (Al-Shami adds:) Abu Hurayra's narration related by al-Hakim who declared it sound, and by al-Bayhaqi, states that the Prophet ﷺ met the spirits of the Prophets. They glorified their Lord, then Ibrahim ﷺ said:

---

[107]Shaykh Muhammad ibn 'Alawi said that this took place before his ascension according to the highest probability, quoting Najm al-Din al-Ghiti who said: "The narrations agree to the fact that the Prophet ﷺ prayed among the other Prophets in Jerusalem before his ascension." This is one of the two possibilities mentioned by al-Qadi 'Iyad. Ibn Hajar said: "This is apparently the case. The second possibility is that he prayed among them after he came down from the heaven, and they came down also." Ibn Kathir also declared the former scenario the sound one. Some said that there is no objection to the possibility that the Prophet ﷺ prayed among them twice, since some of the hadiths mention that he led them in prayer after his ascent.

Praise to Allah ﷻ Who has taken me as His intimate friend, Who has given me an immense kingdom, Who has made me a prayerful Community and one by whom prayer is led, Who has rescued me from the fire and made it cool and safe for me!

Then Musa عليه السلام glorified his Lord and said:

Praise be to Allah ﷻ Who has spoken to me directly, Who has brought to pass the destruction of Fir'awn and the salvation of the Children of Israel at my hands, and Who has made from among my Community a people who guide others through truth and establish justice upon it!

Then Dawud عليه السلام glorified his Lord and said:

Praise be to Allah ﷻ Who has brought me an immense kingdom, Who has softened iron for my hands, and subjected to me the mountains and the birds which laud Him, and has given me wisdom and unmistakable judgment in my speech!

Then Sulayman عليه السلام glorified his Lord and said:

Praise be to Allah ﷻ Who has subjected the winds to my command as well as the devils, so that they did as I wished and constructed for me elevated sanctuaries, images, large bowls the size of ponds, and vessels fixed in their spot [due to their size]! Who has taught me the language of birds and has brought me a part of every good thing! Who has subjected to me the armies of the devils and the birds and has preferred me over many of His believing servants! Who has brought me an immense kingdom which no one after me may possess! And Who has made my kingdom a goodly one wherein there is no reckoning nor punishment!

Then 'Isa ibn Maryam عليه السلام glorified his Lord and said:

Praise be to Allah ﷻ Who has made me His Word! Who has fashioned me after Adam's likeness whom He created out of earth then said to him: Be! and he was. Who has taught me the Book and the Wisdom and the Torah and the Evangel! Who has caused me to heal the blind and the leper and to raise the dead by Allah's permission! Who has raised me and cleansed me and granted me and my mother protection against the cursed devil, so that the devil had no path by which to harm us! (End of al-Shami's addition).

Every Prophet then glorified his Lord in the best of language, and the Prophet ﷺ said:

All of you have glorified their Lord and I am going to glorify Him also:

Al-hamdu lillâh al-ladhî arsalanî rahmatan li al-'âlamîn
wa kâffatan li al-nâsi bashîran wa nadhîrâ
wa anzala 'alayya al-qur'âna fîhi tibyânun li kulli shay'
wa ja'ala ummatî khayra ummatin ukhrijat li al-nâs
wa ja'ala ummatî wasatâ
wa ja'ala ummatî hum al-awwalûna wa al-âkhirun
wa sharaha lî sadrî wa wada'a 'annî wazrî
wa rafa'a lî dhikrî
wa ja'alanî fâtihan khâtimâ!

Praise to Allah Who has sent me
As a mercy to the worlds sent to all without exception,
A bearer of glad tidings and a warner!

Who has caused to descend upon me the Qur'an
In which there is a perfect exposition of all things!
Who has made my Community the best Community
Ever brought out for the benefit of mankind!
Who has made my Community a median and a middle!
Who has made my Community, in truth,
The first and the last of all Communities!
Who has expanded my breast
And relieved me of my burden!
Who has exalted my name,
And made me the Opener and the Sealer!

Upon hearing this Ibrahim عليه السلام said: "In this has Muhammad 🕮 bested you!"

Then they evoked the matter of the Hour and referred it to Ibrahim عليه السلام, but he said: "I have no knowledge of it." They turned to Musa عليه السلام but he said: "I have no knowledge of it." They turned to 'Isa عليه السلام and he said:

As for the time when it shall befall, no one knows it except Allah 🕮. But this is what my Lord has assured me [concerning what precedes it]. The *Dajjâl* or Anti-Christ shall come forth and I will face him with two rods. At my sight he shall melt like lead. Allah 🕮 shall cause his destruction as soon as he sees me. It will be so that the very stones will say: "O Muslim, behind me hides a disbeliever, therefore come and kill him!" And Allah shall cause them all to die.

People shall then return to their countries and nations. At that time Ya'jûj and Ma'jûj [Gog and Magog] shall come out. They shall come from every direction. They shall trample all nations underfoot. What-

ever they come upon, they shall destroy. They shall
drink up every body of water.

At long last the people shall come to me
bewailing about them. At that time I will invoke Allah
ﷻ against them so that He will destroy them and cause
their death until the whole earth will reek of their stench.
Allah ﷻ will then send down rain which shall carry
their bodies away and hurl them into the sea.

I have been assured by my Lord that once all
this takes place then the Hour will be as the pregnant
mother at the last stages of her pregnancy. Her family
does not know when she shall suddenly give birth – by
night or by day. (End of al-Shami's addition)

The Prophet ﷺ then felt the greatest thirst that he had
ever felt, whereupon Gibrîl عليه السلام brought him a vessel of wine
and a vessel of milk. He chose the latter. Gibrîl said: "You have
chosen *fitra* – natural disposition. Had you chosen to drink the
wine, your Community would have strayed from the right way
and none but a few of them would have followed you."[108]

---

[108]The Prophet ﷺ said: "Every child is born with natural disposition
(kullu mawlûdin yûladu 'alâ al-fitra). Then his parents convert him to
Judaism, or Christianity, or Zoroastrianism. It is the same with the
animal which delivers a fully formed *(jam'â')* calf. Do you find that it
is missing part of its facial features *(jad'â')*?" Narrated from Abu
Hurayra by al-Bukhari, Muslim, Abu Dawud, Ahmad, and Malik. Al-
Tirmidhi also narrates it *(hasan sahîh)* but omits the mention of the
animal and narrates the addition: "O Messenger of Allah, what if the
child dies before that?" He replied: "Allah knows best what they would
have done."

The hadith master Murtada al-Zabidi said in his commentary
on al-Ghazali's *Ihya'* entitled *Ithaf al-Sada al-Muttaqin bi Sharh Ihya'
'Ulum al-Din* ("The Gift of the Godwary Masters: Commentary on al-
Ghazali's 'Giving Life to the Sciences of the Religion'"): "The definite

Another narration states: There were three vessels and the third contained water. Gibrîl said: "If you had drunk the water your Community would have perished by drowning."

Another narration states that one of the vessels presented to him contained honey instead of water, and that he then saw the wide-eyed maidens of Paradise at the left of the Rock. He greeted them and they returned his greeting. Then he asked them something and they replied with an answer that cools the eyes.

Then the Prophet 繋 was brought the ladder by which the spirits of the children of Adam 繋 ascend. Creation never saw a more beautiful object. It had alternate stairs of silver and gold and came down from the Highest and Amplest Garden of Paradise, *Janna al-Firdaws*. It was incrusted with pearls and surrounded with angels on its right and left.

The Prophet 繋 began his ascent with Gibrîl 繋 until they reached one of the gates of the nearest heaven called *Bab al-Hafaza*. There an angel stood guard, named Isma'il 繋, who is the custodian of the nearest heaven. He inhabits the wind. He never ascended to the heaven nor descended to earth except on the day that the Prophet 繋 died, blessings and peace upon him. In front of him stood seventy thousand angels, each angel commanding an army of seventy thousand more.

Gibrîl 繋 asked for the gate to be opened. Someone said:

---

case in *al-fitra* indicates that it is universally known and consists in Allah's disposition with which He endows all people. That is, the innate character with which He creates them and which predisposes them to accept Religion and to differentiate between wrong and right." Al-Zabidi, *Ithaf al-Sada al-Muttaqin* (7:233).

– "Who is this?"
– "Gibrîl."
– "Who is with you?"
– "Muhammad."
– "Has he been sent for?"
– "Yes."
– "Welcome to him, from his family! May Allah grant him long life! A brother and deputy, and what an excellent brother and deputy! What an excellent visit this is!"

The gate was opened. When they came in they saw Adam ﷺ the father of humanity, just as he was on the very day Allah ﷺ created him in his complete form.[109] The spirits of the Prophets and of his faithful offspring were being shown to him, whereupon he would say: "A goodly spirit and a goodly soul, put it in the Highest *('illiyyîn)*!" Then the spirits of his disbelieving offspring would be shown to him and he would say: "A foul spirit and a foul soul, put it in the lowest layer of Hell *(sijjîn)*!"

The Prophet ﷺ saw to Adam's right great dark masses and a gate exuding a fragrant smell, and to his left great dark masses and a gate exuding a foul, putrid smell. Whenever Adam ﷺ looked to his right he would smile and be happy, and whenever he looked to his left he would be sad and weep. The Prophet ﷺ greeted him and Adam returned his greeting and said: "Welcome to the righteous son and the righteous Prophet!"

The Prophet ﷺ said: "What is this, O Gibrîl?" He replied: "This is your father Adam ﷺ and the dark throngs are the souls of his children. Those on the right are the people of Paradise and those on the left are the people of the Fire. When-

---

[109]I.e. without passing him through the stages of embryonic formation. The scholars have explained in this sense the hadith "Allah created Adam in his form," narrated from Abu Hurayra by al-Bukhari and Muslim, i.e. in his finished form.

ever he looks to his right he smiles and is glad, and whenever he looks to his left he is sad and weeps. The door to his right is the gate of Paradise. Whenever he sees those of his offspring enter it he smiles happily. The door to his left is the gate of Hell-Fire. Whenever he sees those of his offspring enter it he weeps sadly."

(Al-Shami added:) Then the Prophet ﷺ continued for a little while. He saw a tablespread in which there were pieces of good meat which no one approached, and another tablespread in which were pieces of rotten meat which stank, surrounded by people who were eating it. The Prophet ﷺ asked: "O Gibrîl, who are these?" He replied: "These are those of your Community who abandon what is lawful and proceed to what is unlawful."

(Another version says:) The Prophet ﷺ saw a great deal of people gathered around a tablespread in which was set grilled meat of the best kind one had ever seen. Near the table there was some carrion decaying. The people were coming to the carrion to eat from it, and they were leaving the grilled meat untouched. The Prophet ﷺ asked: "Who are they, O Gibrîl?" He replied: "The adulterers *(al-zunât)*: they make lawful what Allah ﷻ has made unlawful, and they abandon what Allah ﷻ has made lawful for them."

Then the Prophet ﷺ went on for a little while. He saw groups of people who had bellies as large as houses, and there were snakes in them which could be seen through their skins. Every time one of those people stood up he would fall again and he would say: "O Allah, don't make the Hour of Judgment rise yet!" Then they meet the people of Fir'awn on the road and the latter trample them underfoot. The Prophet ﷺ said: "I heard them clamoring to Allah." He asked: "O Gibrîl, who are these?" He replied: "They are those of your Community who eat up usury *(al-ribâ)*. They cannot stand up except in the manner of those whom shaytan touches with possession."

Then the Prophet went on for a little while. He saw groups of people whose lips resembled the lips of camels. Their mouths were being pried open and they would be stoned. One version says: A rock from Hell-Fire was placed in their mouths and then it would come out again from their posteriors. The Prophet said: "I heard them clamoring to Allah." He asked: "O Gibrîl, who are these?" He replied: "They are those of your Community who eat up the property of orphans and commit injustice. They are eating nothing but a fire for their bellies, and they shall be roasted in it."

Then the Prophet went on for a little while. He saw women suspended by their breasts and others hanging upside down. The Prophet said: "I heard them clamoring to Allah." He asked: "Who are these, O Gibrîl?" He replied: "These are the women who commit fornication and then kill their children."

Then the Prophet went on for a little while. He saw groups of people whose sides were being cut off for meat and they were being devoured. They were being told: "Eat, just as you used to eat the flesh of your brother." The Prophet said: "O Gibrîl, who are these?" He replied: "They are the slanderers of your Community who bring shame to others." (End of al-Shami's addition.)

Then the Prophet continued for a little while, and he found the consumers of usury and of the property of orphans, the fornicators and adulterers, and others, in various horrible states like those that have been described or worse.

Then they ascended to the second heaven. Gibrîl asked for the gate to be opened. Someone said:

– "Who is this?"

– "Gibrîl."
– "Who is with you?
– "Muhammad."
– "Has he been sent for?"
– "Yes."
– "Welcome to him, from his family! May Allah grant him long life, a brother and deputy, and what excellent brother and deputy! What an excellent visit this is!"

The gate was opened. When they came in they saw the sons of the two sisters: 'Isa ibn Maryam عليه السلام and Yahya ibn Zakariyya عليه السلام. They resembled each other in clothing and hair. Each had with him a large company of their people. 'Isa was curly-haired, of medium build, leaning towards fair complexion, with hair let down as if he were coming out of the bath. He resembles 'Urwa ibn Mas'ud al-Thaqafi.[110]

---

[110]The martyred Companion 'Urwa ibn Mas'ud al-Thaqafi رضي الله عنه was one of the dignitaries of the town of Ta'if. Ibn Hajar in *al-Isaba* (4:492-493) and Ibn 'Abd al-Barr in *al-Isti'ab* (8:1066-1067) relate that he alone responded to the Prophet's ﷺ invitation to that city by following him and declaring his acceptance of Islam. Then he asked for permission to return to his people and speak to them. The Prophet ﷺ said: "I fear lest they harm you." He said: "They would not even wake me up if they saw me sleeping." Then he returned. When he began to invite them to Islam, they rejected him. One morning as he stood outside his house raising *adhân*, a man shot him with an arrow. As he lay dying he was asked: "What do you think about your death now?" He replied: "It is a gift granted me out of Allah's generosity." When news of this reached the Prophet ﷺ he said: "He is like the man of Yâ Sîn when he came to his people," a reference to the verses **《And there came from the uttermost part of the city a man running. He cried: O my people! Follow those who have been sent! Follow those who ask of you no fee, and who are rightly guided. For what cause should I not serve Him Who has created me, and unto Whom you will be brought back? Shall I take (other) gods in place of Him when, if the Beneficent should wish me any harm, their intercession will avail me naught, nor can they save? Then truly I**

The Prophet 鑾 greeted them and they returned his greeting. Then they said: "Welcome to the righteous brother and the righteous Prophet!" Then they invoked for goodness on his behalf.

After this the Prophet 鑾 and Gibrîl 嫠 ascended to the third heaven. Gibrîl asked for the gate to be opened. Someone said:

- "Who is this?"
- "Gibrîl."
- "Who is with you?
- "Muhammad."
- "Has he been sent for?"
- "Yes."
- "Welcome to him, from his family! May Allah grant him long life, a brother and deputy, and what excellent brother and deputy! What an excellent visit this is!"

The gate was opened. When they came in they saw Yusuf 嫠, and with him stood a large company of his people. The Prophet 鑾 greeted him and he returned his greeting and said: "Welcome to the righteous brother and the righteous Prophet!" Then he invoked for goodness on his behalf.

---

should be in error manifest. Lo! I have believed in your Lord, so hear me. It was said (unto him): Enter Paradise. He said: Would that my people knew With what (munificence) my Lord has pardoned me and made me of the honored ones⟩ (36:20-27). Ibn Hajar also mentions that it is from 'Urwa that Abu Nu'aym narrated – with a weak chain – that the Prophet 鑾 took the women's pledge of allegiance at Hudaybiyya by touching the water of a pail in which they dipped their hands.

Yusuf 雛 had been granted the gift of beauty. One narration states: He was the most handsome creation that Allah 鑩 had ever created and he surpassed people in beauty the way the full moon surpasses all other stars. The Prophet 鑩 asked: "Who is this, O Gibrîl?" He replied: "Your brother Yusuf."

Then they ascended to the fourth heaven. Gibrîl asked for the gate to be opened. Someone said:

– "Who is this?"
– "Gibrîl."
– "Who is with you?
– "Muhammad."
– "Has he been sent for?"
– "Yes."
– "Welcome to him, from his family! May Allah grant him long life, a brother and deputy, and what excellent brother and deputy! What an excellent visit this is!"

The gate was opened. When they came in they saw Idris 雛. Allah 鑩 exalted him to a lofty place. The Prophet 鑩 greeted him and he returned his greeting and said: "Welcome to the righteous brother and the righteous Prophet!" Then he invoked for goodness on his behalf.

Then they ascended to the fifth heaven. Gibrîl asked for the gate to be opened. Someone said:

– "Who is this?"
– "Gibrîl."
– "Who is with you?
– "Muhammad."
– "Has he been sent for?"
– "Yes."

– "Welcome to him, from his family! May Allah grant
him long life, a brother and deputy, and what excellent
brother and deputy! What an excellent visit this is!"

The gate was opened. When they came in they saw
Harun ﷺ. Half of his beard was white and the other half black.
It almost reached his navel due to its length. Surrounding him
were a company of the children of Israel listening to him as he
was telling them a story. The Prophet ﷺ greeted him and he
returned his greeting and said: "Welcome to the righteous
brother and the righteous Prophet!" Then he invoked for goodness on his behalf. The Prophet ﷺ asked: "Who is this, O
Gibrîl?" He replied: "This is the man beloved among his people,
Harun ibn 'Imran."

Then they ascended to the sixth heaven. Gibrîl asked for
the gate to be opened. Someone said:

– "Who is this?"
– "Gibrîl."
– "Who is with you?
– "Muhammad."
– "Has he been sent for?"
– "Yes."
– "Welcome to him, from his family! May Allah grant
him long life, a brother and deputy, and what excellent
brother and deputy! What an excellent visit this is!"

The gate was opened. The Prophet ﷺ passed by
Prophets who had with them less than ten followers in all, while
others had a large company, and others had not even one
follower.

Then he saw a huge dark mass *(sawâd 'azîm)* that was
covering the firmament. He said: "What is this throng?" He was

79

told: "This is Musa and his people. Now raise your head and look." He raised his head and saw another huge dark mass that was covering the firmament from every direction he looked. He was told: "These are your Community, and besides these there are seventy thousand of them that will enter Paradise without giving account."

As they went in the Prophet ﷺ saw Musa ibn 'Imran عليه السلام, a tall man with brown complexion, similar to one of the Shanu'a – the [Yemeni] men of pure lineage and manly virtue – with abundant hair. If he had two shirts on him, still his hair would exceed them. The Prophet ﷺ greeted him and he returned his greeting and said: "Welcome to the righteous brother and the righteous Prophet!" Then he invoked for goodness on his behalf and said: "The people claim that among the sons of Adam I am more honored by Allah than this one, but it is he who is more honored by Allah than me!"

When the Prophet ﷺ reached him Musa عليه السلام wept. He was asked: "What is it that makes you weep?" He replied: "I weep because a child that was sent after me will cause more people to enter Paradise from his Community than will enter from mine. The children of Israel claim that among the children of Adam I am the one most honored by Allah, but here is one man among the children of Adam who has come after me in the world while I am in the next world, and is more honored. If he were only by himself I would not mind, but he has his Community with him!"

Then they ascended to the seventh heaven. Gibrîl asked for the gate to be opened. Someone said:

– "Who is this?"
– "Gibrîl."
– "Who is with you?

– "Muhammad."
– "Has he been sent for?"
– "Yes."
– "Welcome to him, from his family! May Allah grant him long life, a brother and deputy, and what excellent brother and deputy! What an excellent visit this is!"

The gate was opened. The Prophet ﷺ saw Ibrahim عليه السلام the Friend sitting at the gate of Paradise on a throne of gold the back of which was leaning against the Inhabited House *(al-bayt al-ma'mûr)*. With him were a company of his people. The Prophet ﷺ greeted him and he returned his greeting and said: "Welcome to the righteous son and the righteous Prophet!"[111]

Then Ibrahim عليه السلام said: "Order your Community to increase their seedlings of Paradise for its soil is excellent and its land is plentiful." The Prophet said: "What are the seedlings of Paradise?" He replied: *"Lâ hawla wa lâ quwwata illâ billâh al-'alî al-'azîm* – There is no change nor might except with Allah the Exalted, the Almighty!"

(Another version says:) "Convey my greetings to your Community and tell them that Paradise has excellent soil and sweet water, and that its seedlings are:

subhan allâh: Glory to Allah!
wa al-hamdu lillâh: and Praise to Allah!
wa lâ ilâha illallâh: and there is no God but Allah!
wallâhu akbar: and Allah is greatest!

With Ibrahim عليه السلام were sitting a company of people with pristine faces similar to the whiteness of a blank page, and next

---

[111]Shaykh Muhammad ibn 'Alawi said: "*Ma'mûr* means inhabited with the remembrance of Allah and the great number of angels."

to them were people with something in their faces. The latter stood and entered a river in which they bathed. Then they came out having purified some of their hue. Then they entered another river and bathed and came out having purified some more. Then they entered a third river and bathed and purified themselves and their hue became like that of their companions. They came back and sat next to them.

The Prophet ﷺ said: "O Gibrîl, who are those with white faces and those who had something in their hues, and what are these rivers in which they entered and bathed?" He replied: "The ones with white faces are a people who never tarnished their belief with injustice or disobedience; those with something in their hues are a people who would mix good deeds with bad ones, then they repented and Allah relented towards them. As for these rivers, the first is Allah's mercy *(rahmatullâh)*, the second his favor *(ni'matullâh)*, the third **(and their Lord gave them a pure beverage to drink)** *(wa saqâhum rabbuhum sharâban tahûrâ)* (76:21)."

Then the Prophet ﷺ was told: "This is your place and the place of your Community." He saw that his Community were divided into two halves: one half were wearing clothes that seemed as white as a blank page, the other were wearing clothes that seemed the color of ashes or dust. He entered the Inhabited House and those who were wearing the white clothes entered with him. Those that wore ash-colored clothes were no longer able to see him, and yet they were in the best of states. The Prophet ﷺ prayed in the Inhabited House together with those of the believers that were with him.

Every day seventy thousand angels enter the Inhabited House, who shall never return to it until the Day of Resurrection. The angels who have entered it never see it again. This House is exactly superposed to the Ka'ba. If one stone fell from it, it would fall on top of the Ka'ba.

One version states that the presentation of the three vessels, the Prophet's 🌸 choice of the vessel of milk, and Gibrîl's approval took place at this point. (Al-Shami adds:) al-Tabarani cites this hadith with a sound chain: "The night I was taken on a Night-Journey I passed by the heavenly host, and lo and behold! Gibrîl was like the worn-out saddle-cloth on the camel's back from fear of his Lord." One of al-Bazzar's narrations states: "like a saddle-blanket that clings to the ground."[112]

Then the Prophet 🌸 was raised up to the Lote-tree of the Farthest Limit. There ends whatever ascends from the earth before it is seized, and whatever descends from above before it is seized.[113]

---

[112]Shaykh Muhammad ibn 'Alawi said: "Of the same meaning is the hadith *kun hilsan min ahlâsi baytik*, 'Be one of the saddle-blankets of your house,' that is: keep to it in times of dissension." Narrated from Ibn Mas'ud by Abu Dawud in his *Sunan*.

[113]Al-Dardir said: "This is the eighth ascension, meaning that it is the ascension to what is higher than the Lote-tree by means of the eighth step, so that the Prophet reached the top height of its branches in the eighth firmament which is called *al-Kursî* – the Chair or Footstool – which is made of white pearl. This is found in al-Qalyubi, and it is the literal sense of the account. However, it is contradicted by what is mentioned later: 'Then he came to the Kawthar,' because the Kawthar, like the remainder of the rivers, flows from the base of the Tree, not from its top. The account goes on to say after this: 'Then he was raised up to the Lote-tree of the Farthest Limit.' It follows that the raising up to the Lote-tree took place more than once, but this is definitely dubious upon anyone's reflection. I saw in al-Ajhuri's account at this point: 'Then he came to the Lote-tree of the farthest boundary, there ends etc.' and this is correct as it does not signify being raised up. This makes it clear that he 🌸 came to the Tree and saw at its base the rivers – which are soon to be mentioned – and travelled towards the Kawthar. What the narrator said later: 'Then he was raised to the Lote-tree of the

It is a tree from the base of which issue rivers whose water is never brackish,[114] and rivers of milk whose taste does not change after it is drunk, and rivers of wine which brings only pleasure to those who drink it, and rivers of purified honey. Someone on his mount could travel under its shade for seventy years and still not come out of it. The lotus fruit that grows on it resembles the jars of Hijar [near Madina]. Its leaves are shaped like the ears of the she-elephant, and each leaf could wrap up this Community entirely. One version says that one of its leaves could wrap up all creatures.

On top of each leaf there was an angel who covered it with colors which cannot be described. Whenever he covered it by Allah's order it would change. One version says: It would turn into sapphire and chrysolite, the beauty of which is impossible for anyone to praise according to its merit. On it alighted moths of gold.

From the base of the tree issued four [more] rivers: two hidden rivers and two visible ones. The Prophet ﷺ asked: "What are these, O Gibrîl? He replied: "As for the hidden ones, they are two rivers of Paradise. The visible ones are the Nile and the Euphrates."[115]

Farthest Limit etc.' indicates that the eighth ascension took place at that later point and that the present stage is only an exposition of his coming to the base of the Tree which is in the seventh heaven. Another narration states that it is in the sixth heaven. What harmonizes the two is that its base is in the sixth heaven while its branches and trunk are in the seventh."

[114]It does not change in taste, or color, or smell, and the sweat of those who drink it in Paradise has the fragrance of musk.

[115]Ibn Kathir said: "What is meant by this – and Allah knows best – is that these two rivers (the Nile and the Euphrates) resemble the rivers of Paradise in their purity, sweetness, fluidity, and such of their qualities. As the Prophet ﷺ said in the hadith narrated by Abu Hurayra: *al-'ajwa*

(Al-Shami added that one version says): At the base of the tree ran a source called Salsabîl. From it issued two rivers: one is the Kawthar. (The Prophet 🕌 said:) "I saw it flowing impetuously, roaring, at the speed of arrows. Near it were pavilions of pearl *(lu'lu')*, sapphire *(yâqût)*, and chrysolite *(zabarjad)* on top of which nested green birds more delicate than any you have ever seen. On its banks were vessels of gold and silver. It ran over pebbles made of sapphire and emerald *(zumurrud)*. Its water was whiter than milk."

The Prophet 🕌 took one of the vessels and scooped some water and drank. It was sweeter than honey and more fragrant than musk. Gibrîl said to him: "This is the river which Allah 🕌 has given you as a special gift, and the other river is the River of Mercy." The Prophet 🕌 bathed in it and his past and future sins were forgiven. (End of al-Shami's addition.)

(One version says:) At the Lote-tree of the Farthest Limit the Prophet saw Gibrîl (in his angelic form). He had six hundred wings. Every single wing could cover the entire firmament. From his wings embellishments were strewn in all directions, such as rare pearls and sapphires of a kind Allah alone knows. Then the Prophet 🕌 was taken to the Kawthar and entered Paradise. Lo and behold! It contains what no eye has seen, nor ear heard, nor human mind ever imagined. On its gate he saw written:

> *al-sadaqatu bi 'ashrin amthâliha*
> *wa al-qardu bi thamâniyati 'ashara*

---

min al-janna 'Date pastry is from paradise.' That is: it resembles the fruit of Paradise, not that it itself originates in Paradise. If the latter were the actual meaning then the senses would testify to the contrary. Therefore, the meaning which imposes itself is other than that. Similarly, the source of origin of these rivers is on earth."

85

Charity is repaid tenfold, and loan eighteenfold.

The Prophet ﷺ said: "O Gibrîl, how can the loan be more meritorious than charity?" He replied: "Because one asking for charity may still have some need left, while the borrower does not borrow except his need is fulfilled."

The Prophet ﷺ continued to travel until he reached rivers of milk whose taste does not change, and rivers of wine which bring only pleasure to those who drink it, and rivers of honey purified. Overhanging those rivers were domes of hollowed pearl whose circumference is as wide as the Aquarius star.

(Another narration says:) Above the rivers were pommels resembling the hides of humped camels. Its birds were like the Bactrian camel. Upon hearing this, Abu Bakr ﷺ said: "O Messenger of Allah, they are certainly delicate!" The Prophet ﷺ replied: "And daintier to eat yet, and I hope that you shall eat from them."[116]

The Prophet ﷺ then saw the Kawthar and on its banks were domes of hollowed pearl. The soil of its banks was extremely fragrant musk. Then the Fire was shown to him. In it he saw Allah's wrath and His punishment and sanction. Were rocks and iron to be thrown into it the Fire would consume them completely. In it were a people who were eating carrion. The Prophet ﷺ said: "Who are these, O Gibrîl?" He replied: "Those who ate the flesh of people." Then the Prophet ﷺ saw Malik ﷺ, the custodian of the Fire. He was a grim figure whose face

[116]This is an indication of the rank of Abu Bakr in Paradise, as the Prophet's ﷺ hope, like his petition, is granted. Shaykh Muhammad ibn 'Alawi also said: "From all this it can be known that Paradise and the Fire exist already, and that the Lote-tree of the Farthest Boundary is outside Paradise."

expressed anger. The Prophet 鄧 greeted him first. Then the gates of the Fire were closed as he stood outside, and he was raised up beyond the Lote-tree of the Farthest Limit, and a cloud concealed him from everything else, and Gibrîl stayed back.[117]

The Prophet 鄧 was taken up to a point where he heard the scratching of the Pens [writing the divine Decree]. He saw a man who had disappeared into the light of the Throne. He said: "Who is this? Is this an angel?" It was said to him, no. He said: "Is it a Prophet?" Again the answer was no. He said: "Who is it then?" The answer was: "This is a man whose tongue was moist with Allah's remembrance in the world, and his heart was attached to the mosques, and he never incurred the curse of his father and mother."

Then the Prophet 鄧 saw his Lord, the Most Glorious, the Exalted, and he fell prostrate.[118] At that time his Lord spoke to him and said: "O Muhammad!" He replied: "At your service, O Lord!" Allah 鄧 said: "Ask *(sal)*!" The Prophet said:

---

[117]Shaykh Muhammad ibn 'Alawi said: "The Prophet's 鄧 greeting of Malik 鄧 before Malik greeted him first agrees with the subsequent wording of more than one narrator whereby the Prophet 鄧 said: "I greeted him and he returned my greeting and welcomed me, but he did not smile at me," etc. This is found in some of the narrations. However, the correct narration, as the compiler and others have said, is that it is Malik who greeted the Prophet 鄧 first in order to dispel the harshness of his sight since his face showed severity and anger. It is possible to harmonize the two versions with the fact that the Prophet 鄧 saw Malik more than once, so that Malik was first to greet the Prophet 鄧 the first time, as we said, while the Prophet 鄧 was first to greet Malik the second time, in order to dispel estrangement and to inspire familiarity. Know also that the Prophet's 鄧 sight of Malik was not in the same form that those who are being punished see him."
[118]See Part **IV.**

You have taken to Yourself Ibrahim as an intimate friend *(khalîl)*, and You have given him an immense kingdom. You have spoken to Musa directly, and
have given Dawud an immense kingdom and softened
iron and subjected the mountains to him. You have
given Sulayman an immense kingdom, and subjected the
jinn and men and devils to him, as well as the winds,
and You have given him a kingdom the like no one may
have after him. You have taught 'Isa the Torah and the
Evangel, and made him heal those born blind and the
lepers, and raise up the dead with Your permission, and
You have protected him and his mother from the cursed
devil so that the devil had no path by which to harm
them!

Allah ﷻ said: "And I have taken you to Myself as My
beloved and intimate friend *(habîban wa khalîlâ).*" The narrator
said: It is written in the Torah: *Habîbullâh* "Allah's Beloved."[119]
Allah continued:

---

[119]This wording is in the narration from Abu Hurayra by al-Tabari in
his *Tafsir* (15:10). Another wording states: "And I have take you to
Myself as My intimate friend *(khalîlî).* It is written in the Torah:
Muhammadun Habîb al-Rahmân, Muhammad, the Beloved of the
Merciful." Narrated from Abu Hurayra by al-Bazzar in his *Musnad*
with a chain of trustworthy narrators except for a possible unnamed
link as indicated by al-Haythami in *Majma' al-Zawa'id* (1:71-72). Ibn
Kathir cites the latter in his *Tafsir* (3:21). Al-Suyuti in *al-Durr al-
Manthur* said that it is also narrated by Abu Ya'la, Muhammad ibn
Nasr al-Marwazi in *Kitab al-Sala,* Ibn Abi Hatim, Ibn 'Adi, Ibn
Marduyah, and al-Bayhaqi, in commentary of the verse ❴Glorified be
He Who carried His servant by night from the Inviolable Place of
Worship to the Far Distant Place of Worship the neighborhood
whereof We have blessed, that We might show him of Our tokens!
Lo! He, only He, is the Nearer, the Seer❵ (17:1). Both wordings
refute those who claim that it is preferable to call the Prophet ﷺ
Khalîlullâh rather than *Habîbullâh,* as the latter clearly applies only to
him in the *Umma,* whereas the former applies both to Ibrahim ﷺ and

I have sent you for all people without exception, a bearer of glad tidings and a warner.

I have expanded your breast for you and relieved you of your burden and exalted your name, as I am not mentioned except you are mentioned with Me.

I have made your Community the best Community ever brought out for the benefit of mankind.

I have made your Community a mean and a middle.

I have made your Community in truth the first and the last of all Communities.

I have made public address *(al-khutba)* impermissible for your Community unless they first witness that you are My servant and Messenger

I have placed certain people in your Community with Evangels for hearts.[120]

I have made you the first Prophet created and the last one sent and the first one heard in My court.

I have given you Seven of the Oft-Repeated which I gave to no other Prophet before you.[121]

I have given you the last verses of Sura al-Baqara which constitute a treasure from under My Throne which I gave to no other Prophet before you.

I have given you the Kawthar.

I have given you eight lots: Islam, Emigration *(al-hijra)*, Jihad, Charity *(al-sadaqa)*, Fasting Ramadan,

---

to him 🕌 as stated in the hadith narrated from Ibn Mas'ud by al-Tirmidhi *(hasan sahîh)*: "Verily, your Companion – i.e. himself – is Allah's intimate friend." This holds true regardless of the weak chain of the narration from Ibn 'Abbas narrated by Tirmidhi *(gharîb)* and Darimi whereby the Prophet 🕌 said: "Lo! I am Allah's Beloved, and I say this without pride."
[120]I.e. repositories of Allah's Book.
[121]I.e. Sura al-Fatiha.

Ordering Good, and Forbidding Evil; and the day I
created the heavens and the earth I made obligatory
upon you and upon your Community fifty prayers:
therefore establish them, you and your Community.

(Al-Shami added:) Abu Hurayra said that Allah's Messenger said 🕌:

> My Lord has preferred me over everyone else
> *(faddalanî rabbî)*.
> He has sent me as a mercy to the worlds and to
> all people without exception, a bearer of glad tidings and
> a warner.
> He has thrown terror into the hearts of my ene-
> mies at a distance of a month's travel.
> He has made spoils of war lawful for me while
> they were not lawful for anyone before me.
> The entire earth has been made a ritually pure
> place of prostration for me.
> I was given the words that open, those that
> close, and those that are comprehensive in meaning.[122]
> My Community was shown to me and there is
> none of the followers and the followed but he is known
> to me.
> I saw that they would come to a people that
> wear hair-covered sandals.[123]
> I saw that they would come to a people of large
> faces and small eyes as if they had been pierced with a
> needle.
> Nothing of what they would face in the future
> has been kept hidden from me.

---

[122]I.e. I was given the apex of eloquence.
[123]I.t. untanned sandals.

And I have been ordered to perform fifty prayers daily.

And he has been given three particular merits: He is the Master of Messengers *(sayyid al-mursalîn)*, the Leader of the Godwary *(imâm al-muttaqîn)*, and the Chief of Those with Signs of Light on Their Faces and Limbs *(qâ'id al-ghurr al-muhajjalîn)*. (End of al-Shami's addition.)

One narration says: The Prophet 🕌 was given the five daily prayers and the last verses of Sura al-Baqara. For his sake, whoever of his Community does not associate anything with Allah 🕌 is forgiven even the mortal sins.

Then the cloud that cloaked him was dispelled and Gibrîl 🕌 took him by the hand and sped away with him until he reached Ibrahim 🕌, who did not say anything. Then the Prophet 🕌 reached Musa 🕌 who asked: "What did you do, O Muhammad? What obligations did your Lord impose on you and your Community?" He replied: "He imposed fifty prayers every day and night on me and my Community." Musa 🕌 said: "Return to your Lord and ask Him to lighten your burden and that of your Community for in truth your Community will not be able to carry it. Verily I myself have experienced people's dispositions before you. I tested the Children of Israel and took the greatest pains to hold them to something easier than this, but they were too weak to carry it and they abandoned it. Those of your Community are even weaker in their bodies and constitutions, and in their hearts, their sight, and their hearing."

The Prophet 🕌 turned to Gibrîl 🕌 to consult him. The latter indicated to him that yes, if he wished, then return. The Prophet sped back until he reached the Tree and the cloud cloaked him and he fell prostrate. Then he said: "My Lord, make lighter the burden of my Community for verily they are the weakest of all Communities." He replied: "I have removed five prayers from their obligation."

Then the cloud was dispelled and the Prophet ﷺ returned to Musa عليه السلام and told him: "He has removed five prayers from my obligation." He replied: "Go back to your Lord and ask him to make it less, for in truth your Community will not be able to carry that." The Prophet ﷺ did not cease to go back and forth between Musa and his Lord, while Allah ﷻ each time reduced it by five prayers, until Allah ﷻ said: "O Muhammad!" The Prophet said: "At Your service, O Lord!" He said:

> Let them be five prayers every day and night, and let every prayer count as ten. That makes fifty prayers. This word of Mine shall not be changed nor shall My Book be abrogated. Let whoever is about to perform a good deed, even if he does not ultimately do it, receive the reward of doing it, while if he does it, he shall receive it tenfold. Let whoever is about to commit a bad deed, and he does not ultimately do it, let not anything be written against him, while if he does it, let one misdeed be written against him.

Then the cloud was dispelled and the Prophet ﷺ returned to Musa عليه السلام and told him: "He has removed five prayers from my obligation." He replied: "Go back to your Lord and ask him to make it less, for in truth your Community will not be able to carry that." The Prophet ﷺ said: "I have gone back again to my Lord until I feel shy from Him. Rather, I accept and submit." At this a herald called out: "I have decreed My obligation and have reduced the burden of My servants." Musa عليه السلام then said to the Prophet ﷺ: "Return back down in the name of Allah."

The Prophet 🕌 did not pass a throng of angels except they said to him: "You must practice cupping *('alayka bi al-hijâma)*," and in another version: "Order your Community to apply cupping."[124]

As the Prophet 🕌 was descending he asked Gibrîl 🕌: "Why did I not see any of the people of heaven except they welcomed me and smiled at me except one: I greeted him and he greeted me back and welcomed me, but he did not smile at me?" He replied: "That was Malik 🕌 the custodian of the Fire. He never smiled once since the day he was created. If he had ever smiled for anyone, it would have been you."

When the Prophet 🕌 reached the nearest heaven he looked below it and he saw a dense cloud of smoke filled with clamor. He asked: "What is this, O Gibrîl?" He replied: "These are the devils that swarm over the eyes of human beings so that they will not think about the dominions of the heavens and the earth, or else they would have seen wonders."

Then he mounted the Burâq again (which he had tied in Jerusalem) and departed. He passed by a caravan of the Quraysh in such-and-such a place (the narrator forgot the name) and saw a camel upon which were tied two containers, a black one and a white one. When he came face to face with the caravan there was a stampede in which the caravan turned around and that camel was thrown down to the ground and its freight broke.

Then the Prophet 🕌 passed by another caravan that had lost one of its camels which the tribe of So-and-so had rounded up. The Prophet 🕌 greeted them and one of them said: "This is

---

[124]Cupping is the process of drawing blood from the body by scarification (scratches or superficial incisions in the skin) and the application of a cupping glass (in which a partial vacuum is created, as by heat) without scarification, as for relieving internal congestion.

the voice of Muhammad!" after which the Prophet 🕋 returned to his Companions in Mecca shortly before morning.

When morning came he remained alone and, knowing that people would belie him, sat despondently. Allah's enemy, Abu Jahl, was passing by and he approached and sat down next to him, saying by way of mockery: "Has anything happened?" The Prophet 🕋 replied: "Yes." Abu Jahl said: "And what is that?" The Prophet 🕋 replied: "I was taken on a Night-Journey last night." Abu Jahl said: "Where to?" The Prophet 🕋 replied: "To the Hallowed House." Abu Jahl said: "Then you woke up here among us?" He replied: "Yes."

Abu Jahl decided not to belie the Prophet 🕋, fearing that the latter would deny having said this to him if he went and told the people of Mecca, so he said: "What do you think if I called your people here? Will you tell them what you just told me?" The Prophet 🕋 said yes. Abu Jahl cried out: "O assembly of the Children of Ka'b ibn Lu'ay, come hither!" People left their gatherings and came until they all sat next around the two of them. Abu Jahl said: "Tell your people what you just told me." Allah's Messenger 🕋 said: "I was taken on a Night-Journey last night." They said: "To where?" The Prophet 🕋 replied: "To the Hallowed House." They said: "Then you woke up here among us?" He replied: "Yes." There was no one left except he clapped his hands, or held his head in amazement, or clamored and considered it an enormity.

Al-Mut'im ibn 'Adi[125] said: "All of your affair before today was bearable, until what you said today. I bear witness that you are a liar *(anâ ashhadu annaka kâdhibun)*! We strike the flanks of the she-camels for one month to reach the Hallowed House, then for another month to come back, and you claim that

---

[125]He died a disbeliever.

you went there in one night! By al-Lat, by al-'Uzza! I do not believe you."

Abu Bakr 🌸 said: "O Mut'im! It is an evil thing you said to your brother's son when you faced him thus and declared him a liar! As for me, I bear witness that he spoke the truth *(anâ ashhadu annahu sâdiqun)*!"

The people said: "O Muhammad, describe the Hallowed House for us. How is it built, what does it look like, how near is it to the mountain?" There were some among them who had travelled there. He began to describe it for them: "Its structure is like this, its appearance like this, its proximity to the mountain is such-and-such," and he did not stop describing it to them until he began to experience doubts about the description. He was seized with an anxiety he had not felt before, whereupon he was brought to the mosque itself [in Jerusalem] on the spot and saw it in front of him. He was placed outside the gate of 'Aqil or 'Iqal. The people said: "How many gates does the mosque have?" He had not counted them before. He looked at the gates and began to count them one by one, informing them. All the while Abu Bakr was saying: "You have spoken the truth. You have spoken the truth. I bear witness that you are the Messenger of Allah *(sadaqta sadaqta ashhadu annaka rasûlullâh)*."

The people said: "As for the description, then, by Allah, he is correct." They turned to Abu Bakr and said: "But do you believe what he said, that he went last night to the Hallowed House and came back before morning?" He replied: "Yes, and I do believe him regarding what is farther than that. I believe the news of heaven he brings, whether in the space of a morning or in that of an evening journey *(na'am innî la usaddiquhu fîmâ huwa ab'adu min dhâlika usaddiqu bi khabari al-samâ'i fî ghudwatin aw rawha)*." Because of this Abu Bakr was named *al-Siddîq*: the Trusting and Truthful.

95

Then they said: "O Muhammad, tell us about our caravans!" He replied: "I saw the caravan of the tribe of So-and-so
as I was coming back. They had lost one of their camels and
were searching for it everywhere. I reached their mounts and
there was no one with them. I found a water bottle and I drank
from it."[126]

"Then I reached the caravan of the tribe of So-and-so in
such-and-such a place. I saw a red camel carrying one black con-
tainer and one white one. When I came face to face with the
caravan there was a stampede and that camel fell and its freight
broke. Then I reached the caravan of the tribe of So-and-so in al-
Tan'im. It was headed by a grayish camel on which was a black
hair-cloth and two blackish containers and here are the [three]
caravans about to reach you from the mountain pass." They said:
"When will they arrive?" He replied: "On the fourth day of the
week." On that day the Quraysh came out, expecting the caravans. The day passed and they did not arrive. The Prophet 🌸
made an invocation and the day was extended one more hour
during which the sun stood still, and the caravans came.

They went to meet the riders and asked them: "Did you
lose a camel?" They said yes. They asked the second caravan:
"Did one red camel of yours shatter her freight?" They said yes.
They asked [the first caravan]: "Did anyone lose a water bottle?"

---

[126]Shaykh Muhammad ibn 'Alawi said: "Doubt has been raised about
this report on the basis of the question how could he allow himself to
drink the water without permission from its owner? The answer is that
he acted according to the custom of the Arabs whereby they never
refuse milk to whomever passes by and takes it, *a fortiori* water, and
they used to instruct the herdsmen not to prevent wayfarers from taking
milk from the herd (i.e. without asking the owner), and this applies
even more to water. Furthermore, the Prophet comes before the Believers' own selves and properties, and this applies even more to the unbe-
lievers."

One man said: "I did, by Allah, I had prepared it but none of us drank it nor was it spilled on the ground!" At this they accused the Prophet of sorcery and said: "al-Walid spoke the truth."[127]

---

[127]Ibn Hisham narrates in his *Sira* that when the Meccan fair was due, a number of the Quraysh came to al-Walid ibn al-Mughira, who was a man of some standing, and he addressed them in those words: "The time of the fair has come round again and representatives of the Arabs will come to you and they will have heard about this fellow of yours, so agree upon one opinion without dispute so that none will give the lie to the other." They replied: "You give us your opinion about him." He said: "No, you speak and I will listen." They said: "He is a *kâhin* (seer or giver of oracles)." He said: "By Allah, he is not that, for he has not the unintelligent murmuring and rhymed speech of the *kâhin*." "Then he is possessed," they said. "No, he is not that," he said, "we have seen possessed ones, and here is no choking, spasmodic movements and whispering." "Then he is a poet," they said. "No, he is no poet, for we know poetry in all its forms and meters." "Then he is a sorcerer." "No, we have seen sorcerers and their sorcery, and here is no blowing and no knots." "Then what are we to say, O Abu 'Abd al-Shams?" they asked. He replied: "By Allah, his speech is sweet, his root is a palm-tree whose branches are fruitful, and everything you have said would be known to be false. The nearest thing to the truth is your saying that he is a sorcerer, who has brought a message by which he separates a man from his father, or from his brother, or from his wife, or from his family."

At this point they left him, and began to sit on the paths which men take when they come to the fair. They warned everyone who passed them about the Prophet's 🖌 doings. Allah revealed concerning al-Walid:

{Leave Me to deal with him whom I created lonely,
and then bestowed upon him ample means,
and sons abiding in his presence
and made life smooth for him.
Yet he desires that I should give more.
Nay, for lo! He has been stubborn to Our revelations.
On him I shall impose a fearful doom.
For lo! He did consider; then he planned –
Self-destroyed is he, how he planned!
Again, self-destroyed is he, how he planned! –
Then looked he,

97

Then Allah revealed the verse:

Wa mâ ja'alnâ al-ru'yâ al-latî araynâka
illâ fitnatan li al-nâs

❴We appointed not the vision which We showed you
but as a test for mankind❵ (17:60).

The account is finished with praise to Allah and by His grace. May Allah send blessings and utmost, abundant greetings upon our Master Muhammad and his Family and Companions, and praise belongs to Allah the Lord of the worlds!

Then frowned he and showed displeasure.
Then turned he away in pride
and said: This is naught else than magic from of old;
This is naught else than speech of mortal man.
Him shall I fling unto the burning.❵ (74:11-26)

III.
The Immense Merits of *al-Shâm*

The Arabic word *al-Shâm* has been left untranslated for lack of an English equivalent. It is originally written and pronounced *al-Sha'm* and means "the North" with relation to the Hijaz, covering the lands of present-day Syria, Palestine, Lebanon, and Jordan from the Euphrates to Sinai. Ibn Hibban said: "*Al-Shâm* begins at Bâlis [East of Aleppo] and ends at 'Arish Misr [at the border of Egypt]."[128] The lexical and geographical inclusion of al-Quds (Jerusalem) in *al-Shâm* in the language of the Arabs is established by the narration of Salman al-Farisi's question to the Christians of Persia: "Where is the origin of this religion?" They replied: "In *al-Shâm*."[129] In modern usage *al-Shâm* often means old Damascus. The Arabic term for the latter is *Dimashq*, which is cited in the authentic hadith.[130]

I.   In the Noble Qur'an

1. Allah ﷻ blessed the land of *Shâm* when He said ❨**Glorified be He Who carried His servant by night from the**

---

[128]In *Sahih Ibn Hibban* (16:294). Bâlis is sixty miles East of Aleppo, at the South-East bend of the Euphrates, while 'Arish Misr is the first Egyptian town on the side of *Shâm*, on the Mediterranean coast as defined in *Mu'jam al-Buldan*. Al-Suyuti in *al-Durr al-Manthur* mentions that Ibn 'Asakir narrates something similar from the *Tâbi'î* Abu al-Aghdash. This definition is confirmed by the report narrated from Ka'b al-Ahbar below (p. 101).

[129]Narrated as part of a very long hadith by Ahmad in his *Musnad* and al-Tabarani, both with sound chains as stated by al-Haythami in *Majma' al-Zawa'id*, and by al-Bazzar in his *Musnad*.

[130]Cf. below, Part I #9 and Part VII #14, 23, 26, 27, and 36.

Inviolable Place of Worship to the Far Distant Place of
Worship the neighborhood whereof We have blessed,
that We might show him of Our tokens! Lo! He, only He,
is the Nearer, the Seer⟩ (17:1).

The Prophet 🌸 said: "I was brought the Burâq, a tall white
beast, bigger than a donkey but smaller than a mule. He could
place his hooves at the farthest boundary of his gaze. I mounted
it until I arrived at the Hallowed House *(Bayt al-Maqdis)*. I tied
it at the ring where the Prophets tied it before him. I entered the
mosque and prayed two *rak'as* there.[131]

Other narrations of the hadith of *isrâ'* and *mi'raj* state that
the following took place during the Prophet's 🌸 flight on top of
the Burâq:

Gibrîl said: "Alight and pray here." The Prophet 🌸 did
so then remounted. Gibrîl said: "Do you know where you
prayed?" He said no. Gibrîl said: "You prayed in Madyan[132]
at the tree of Musa."[133] The Burâq continued his lightning
flight, then Gibrîl said: "Alight and pray here." He did so
then remounted, then Gibrîl said: "Do you know where you
prayed?" He said no. Gibrîl said: "You prayed at the
mountain of Sînâ' where Allah addressed Musa." Then he
reached a land where the palaces of *al-Shâm* became visible
to him. Gibrîl said to him: "Alight and pray." He did so and
remounted, then the Burâq continued his lightning flight and
Gibrîl said: "Do you know where you prayed?" He said no.
Gibrîl said: "You prayed in Bayt Lahm, where 'Isa ibn
Maryam was born."... He continued travelling until he

---

[131]Narrated as part of a long hadith from Anas by Muslim and Ahmad.
[132]A city on the shore of the Red Sea bordering Tabuk near the valley
of Shu'ayb.
[133]The tree under which Musa 🌸 rested from fatigue and hunger
during his flight from Fir'awn.

reached the city of the Hallowed House and he entered it by its Southern gate. He dismounted the Burâq and tied it at the gate of the mosque, using the ring by which the Prophets tied it before him. "We entered the mosque from a gate through which the sun and the moon could be seen when they set. I prayed in the mosque for as long as Allah wished."[134]

The commentaries are unanimous in adducing the Prophet's ﷺ reports whereby ❨the **Far Distant Place of Worship the neighborhood whereof We have blessed**❩ is Allah's sanctuary in al-Quds in *Shâm*.[135] Ka'b al-Ahbar said: "Allah has blessed *al-Shâm* from the Euphrates to al-'Arish [Egypt's border]."[136]

2. Allah ﷺ also said ❨**And We caused the folk who were devised to inherit the eastern parts of the land and the western parts thereof which We had blessed**❩ (7:137), meaning *Shâm*, as narrated from the authorities in *tafsîr* among the *Tâbi'în*.[137]

---

[134]Narrated as part of a long hadith from Anas by al-Nasa'i with a sound chain and from Shaddad ibn Aws by al-Bayhaqi who declared it sound in *Dala'il al-Nubuwwa* (2:355-357), and by al-Tabarani in *al-Kabir* and al-Bazzar with a sound chain as indicated by Haythami in *Majma' al-Zawa'id*. See Ibn Hajar's *Mukhtasar* (1:90-91 #32).

[135]See al-Suhayli, *al-Ta'rif wa al-I'lam fî ma Ubhima fî al-Qur'an min al-Asma' wa al-A'lam* (p. 96) and the *Tafsirs* of Abu al-Su'ud (5:155), Ibn Kathir (3:22-24), al-Jalalayn (p. 365), *al-Durr al-Manthur* (5:182, 5:195, 5:222), al-Tabari (15:5), al-Wahidi (2:627), al-Nahhas (4:119), etc. Also al-Mubarakfuri, *Tuhfa* (8:450).

[136]In al-Suyuti, *Mufhimat al-Aqran fî Mubhamat al-Qur'an* (p. 21).

[137]Narrated from al-Hasan and Qatada by 'Abd al-Razzaq in his *Musannaf*, 'Abd ibn Humayd in his *Musnad*, al-Tarabi in his *Tafsir*, Ibn al-Mundhir, Ibn Abi Hatim, Abu al-Shaykh, and Ibn 'Asakir as mentioned in al-Suyuti's *al-Durr al-Manthur* and Ibn 'Abd al-Salam in *Targhib Ahl al-Islam* (p. 13-14).

3. Allah ﷻ also said 〈And We verily did allot unto the
   Children of Israel a beautiful abode *(mubawwa'a sidq)*,
   and provided them with good things〉 (10:93). The
   scholars of the *Tâbi'în* explained the beautiful abode to
   mean *Shâm*.[138]

4. Allah ﷻ also said 〈And We rescued him [Ibrahim] and
   Lot (and brought them) to the land which We have
   blessed for (all) peoples〉 (21:71) meaning *Shâm* according
   to the *Salaf* as reported by the commentators.[139]

5. Allah ﷻ also said 〈And unto Solomon (We subdued) the
   wind in its raging. It set by His command toward the
   land which We had blessed〉 (21:81), meaning *Shâm*.[140] Ibn
   'Abd al-Salam said that the scholars differed whether this
   blessing consisted in the presence of the Prophets and
   Messengers, or with the abundance of harvests and water.[141]

6. Allah ﷻ also said 〈And We set, between them and the
   towns which We had blessed, towns easy to be seen, and
   We made the stage between them easy, (saying): Travel

---

[138]Narrated from Qatada, al-Dahhak, and Ibn Zayd by Ibn al-Mundhir
as stated by al-Suyuti in *Mufhimat al-Aqran fi Mubhamat al-Qur'an* (p.
115) and Ibn 'Abd al-Salam in *Targhib Ahl al-Islam* (p. 14). See the
Tafsirs of Abu al-Su'ud (4:174), al-Jalalayn (p. 281), *al-Durr al-
Manthur* (4:389), al-Tabari (11:166-167), 'Abd al-Razzaq (2:297), Ibn
al-Jawzi (4:62), al-Shawkani (2:485), al-Nahhas (3:316), etc.

[139]See the *Tafsirs* of Abu al-Su'ud (6:77), Ibn Kathir (3:186), al-
Jalalayn (p. 427), *al-Durr al-Manthur* (5:642-643), al-Tabari (11:166,
17:45-47), al-Qurtubi (11:305), al-Wahidi (2:720), Ibn al-Jawzi
(5:368), al-Shawkani (3:416), etc.

[140]See the *Tafsirs* of Abu al-Su'ud (6:80), al-Jalalayn (p. 428), al-
Tabari (17:55), al-Qurtubi (11:322), Ibn al-Jawzi (5:370-374), al-
Shawkani (3:419) etc.

[141]Ibn 'Abd al-Salam, *Targhib* (p. 13).

in them safely both by night and day**)** (34:18). The early
scholars have identified those blessed towns as *Shâm*.[142]

7. Allah ﷻ also swore **(By the fig and the olive, By Mount
    Sînâ)** (95:1-2), meaning by "the fig" *al-Shâm* and by "the
    olive" Palestine, which is also in *Shâm*, as is Sînâ.[143] Each of
    these three symbols and the places they stand for refers in
    turn to a Prophet, respectively Ibrahim ﷽, 'Isa ﷽, and
    Musa ﷽.

8. Allah's mention of "the first gathering" in the verse **(He it is
    Who has caused those of the People of the Scripture who
    disbelieved to go forth from their homes unto the first
    gathering)** (59:2) is an allusion to the second and final
    gathering, both of which take place in *Shâm*.[144]

9. The land of refuge for 'Isa ibn Maryam ﷽ and his mother
    in the verse **(And We made the son of Mary and his
    mother a portent, and We gave them refuge on a height
    (rabwa), a place of flocks and water springs)** (23:50) was

---

[142]See the *Tafsirs* of Abu al-Su'ud (7:128), Ibn Kathir (3:534), al-
Tha'alibi (3:244), al-Jalalayn (p. 566), *al-Durr al-Manthur* (6:692), al-
Tabari (22:83-84), al-Qurtubi (14:289), al-Wahidi (2:882), Mujahid
(2:525), Ibn al-Jawzi (6:448), al-Shawkani (4:321), al-Nahhas (5:410)
etc.
[143]See the *Tafsirs* of Abu al-Su'ud (9:174), Ibn Kathir (4:527), al-
Jalalayn (p. 813), *al-Durr al-Manthur* (8:554-555), al-Tabari (30:239),
'Abd al-Razzaq (3:382), al-Qurtubi (20:111), al-Wahidi (2:1214), Ibn
al-Jawzi (9:168-170), al-Shawkani (5:464-465), etc. and al-Bakri's
Mu'jam ma Ustu'jam (3:898).
[144]See the *Tafsirs* of al-Jassas (5:316), Abu al-Su'ud (8:225), al-
Tha'alibi (4:281-282), al-Jalalayn (p. 730), *al-Durr al-Manthur*
(1:730), al-Tabari (28:28-29), 'Abd al-Razzaq (3:282), al-Qurtubi
(18:2), al-Wahidi (2:1080), Ibn al-Jawzi (8:204), al-Shawkani (5:195,
5:199), etc. and al-Hakim (1990 ed. 2:525). See also the report cited
below (#28).

Damascus according to Ibn 'Abbas, 'Abd Allah ibn Salam, Sa'id ibn al-Musayyib, and al-Hasan al-Basri.[145]

10. Allah's ﷻ statement ⟨**many columned Iram, The like of which was not created in the lands**⟩ (89:7-8) was explained by Bishr ibn al-Harith – Bishr al-Hafi – to refer to *Shâm*.[146]

---

[145]Cf. Ibn Abi Shayba in his *Musannaf* (6:409) with a sound chain to Sa'id ibn al-Musayyib, al-Suyuti in *Mufhamat al-Aqran* (p. 148), al-Haythami in *Majma' al-Zawa'id* (7:72), Ibn 'Abd al-Salam in *Targhib Ahl al-Islam* (p. 27), and the *Tafsirs* of Abu al-Su'ud (6:137), Ibn Kathir (3:247), al-Thawri (p. 216), *al-Durr al-Manthur* (6:101-102), al-Tabari (18:26), 'Abd al-Razzaq (3:45), al-Qurtubi (12:126), al-Wahidi (2:748), Ibn al-Jawzi (5:476), al-Shawkani (3:486-487), al-Nahhas (4:461-462), etc. as well as Yaqut's *Mu'jam al-Buldan* (2:464) and al-Bakri's *Mu'jam ma Ustu'jam* (2:637).

One narration of this commentary has a chain from Ibn al-Musayyib up to 'Abd Allah ibn Salam but its authenticity was questioned by Ibn Abi 'Asim (d. 287) in his *'Ilal al-Hadith* (2:65-66) on the grounds that none of the authorities went further up than Ibn al-Musayyib. However, the hadith master Abu Muhammad al-Ramahurmuzi's (d. 362) narration in *al-Muhaddith al-Fasil Bayn al-Rawi wa al-Wa'i* ("The Hadith Scholar That Differentiates Between Narrators and Containers") (p. 475) does narrate it up to 'Abd Allah ibn Salam with his chain, and both Ibn Kathir in his *Tafsir* (3:247) and al-Qurtubi in his (12:126) mention Ibn Salam's narration. Note that al-Dhahabi lauded al-Ramahurmuzi's book in his *Siyar* (1996 ed. 12:233) and related that al-Silafi carried it wherever he went. Dr. Nur al-Din 'Itr pointed out in a class communication that it was the first comprehensive book on hadith science ever written, second to which came the works of al-Hakim, al-Khatib, and Ibn al-Salah.

Another narration raises this commentary to the Prophet ﷺ from Abu Umama as narrated by Ibn 'Asakir in *Tarikh Dimashq* (1:192), Tammam al-Razi in *al-Fawa'id* (2:11), al-Raba'i in *Fada'il al-Sham wa Dimashq* (p. 37), and al-'Ajluni in *Kashf al-Khafa'* (1:544). However, its chain is very weak due to Maslama ibn 'Ali who is discarded as a narrator *(matrûk)*.

[146]Narrated from al-Maqbiri by al-Tabari in his *Tafsir* (30:111) and others.

VII.   In the Noble Hadith

The Prophet ﷺ called *al-Shâm* the purest of Allah's lands, the place where Religion, belief and safety are found in the time of dissension, and the home of the saints for whose sake Allah sends sustenance to the people and victory to Muslims over their enemies. The following is a list of hadiths relevant to the immense merits of *al-Shâm*:

11. The Prophet ﷺ said: "Blessings to *al-Shâm*, blessings to *al-Shâm*, blessings to *al-Shâm*!" *(yâ tûbâ li al-Shâm)*. They asked why and he replied: "Because the wings of the angels of the Merciful are lowered over it."[147]

Ibn 'Abd al-Salam said: "This is an allusion to the fact that Allah ﷻ has put certain angels in charge of guarding *Shâm* and protecting it. This is in agreement with the hadith of 'Abd Allah ibn Hawala [#18] that states that they [the people of *Shâm*] are under Allah's guarantee *(kafâla)* and His care."[148]

---

[147]Narrated from Zayd ibn Thabit al-Ansari by al-Tirmidhi in his *Sunan (hasan gharîb)* with a fair chain because of Yahya ibn Ayyub al-Ghafiqi who is *sadûq* as in al-Arna'ut and Ma'ruf's *al-Tahrir* (4:78 #7511); Ahmad with two chains, one of which is sound according to Ibn al-Qayyim in his commentary on Abu Dawud's *Sunan* (7:115), the other is a fair chain because of 'Abd Allah ibn Lahi'a; al-Hakim (2:229; 1990 ed. 2:249) who said it is *sahîh* and al-Dhahabi concurred; al-Bayhaqi in the *Shu'ab* (2:432); Ibn Abi Shayba in his *Musannaf* (4:218, 6:409); Ibn Hibban in his *Sahih* (16:293) with a sound chain meeting Muslim's criterion according to Shaykh Shu'ayb Arna'ut; and al-Tabarani in *al-Kabir* (5:158 #4935) with a sound chain according to al-Haythami in *Majma' al-Zawa'id* (10:60) and al-Mundhiri in *al-Targhib* (1997 ed. 4:30).
[148]Ibn 'Abd al-Salam, *Targhib Ahl al-Islam* (p. 21).

12. The Prophet ﷺ said: "The heartland of the Abode of Islam is *al-Shâm.*" *('Uqr dâr al-islâm al-shâm.)* [149] A longer version states that Salama ibn Nufayl al-Hadrami came to the Prophet ﷺ and said: "I have fattened the horses and laid down arms, for war has rested its burdens and there is no more fighting." The Prophet ﷺ said: "Now has fighting come! There shall not cease to be a group in my Community that shall remain victorious over all people. Allah shall cause the hearts of some to go astray and those shall fight them and receive from them Allah's sustenance, until Allah's command comes to pass as they are in that state. Lo! Verily, the heartland of the Believers is *al-Shâm ('uqr dâr al-mu'minîn al-shâm),* and immense good remains tied to the forelocks of horses until the Day of Resurrection." [150]

Ibn 'Abd al-Salam said: "In this hadith the Prophet ﷺ informed us of the apostasy that would take place on the part of those whose hearts Allah would cause to go astray, and the

---

[149]Narrated from Salama ibn Nufayl by al-Tabarani in *al-Kabir* (7:53 #6358) with a sound chain as indicated by al-Haythami in *Majma' al-Zawa'id* (10:60).
[150]Narrated from Salama ibn Nufayl by Ahmad with a fair chain, al-Nasa'i with a sound *(sahîh)* chain, Ibn Sa'd in his *Tabaqat* (7:427-428), and from al-'Irbad ibn Sariya and al-Nuwwas ibn Sam'an by Ibn 'Asakir in his *Tarikh* (1:70, 1:105-106). A forged *mursal* report narrated from the *Tâbi'î* Kathir ibn Murra al-Hadrami by Nu'aym ibn Hammad in *Kitab al-Fitan* (1:254) states that the Prophet ﷺ said: "Lo! Verily, the heartland of the Abode of Islam is *al-Shâm.* Allah leads to it the quintessence of His servants. None earnestly desires to live in it except a beneficiary of divine mercy, and none earnestly desires to live away from it except one seduced by sin. Allah trains His gaze upon it since the beginning of time until the end of time, with shade and rain. Even if He makes its people needy of money, He never made them needy of bread nor water." Its chain contains Sa'id ibn Sinan who is discarded as a narrator because of his forgeries, but I cited it because its last sentence is true from general obervation, and its first two sentences are confirmed in sound narrations. See also below, hadith **#38.**

fighting against the apostates. In his telling us about residing in
Shâm there is a sign that to live there consists in waging war for
Allah's sake, and news that *Shâm* shall remain a fortified
borderline city until the Day of Resurrection. We have witnessed
this, for the outer borders of *Shâm* are permanent front lines."[151]

13. Strengthened by the above report is that of the Prophet's ﷺ
    saying: "The people of *Shâm*, their spouses, their offspring,
    and their male and female servants are garrisoned for Allah's
    sake *(murâbitûn)*. Therefore, whoever takes up residence in
    one of the cities of *Shâm*, he is in a garrison-post or fortified
    borderline city and he is a *mujâhid*."[152]

14. The Prophet ﷺ is also related to say: "A party of my
    Community shall not cease to fight at the gates of Damascus
    and its surroundings and at the gates of *Bayt al-Maqdis* and
    its surroundings. The betrayal or desertion of whoever de-
    serts them shall not harm them in the least. They shall
    remain victorious, standing for truth, until the Hour rises."[153]

---

[151]Ibn 'Abd al-Salam, *Targhib Ahl al-Islam* (p. 20).
[152]Narrated from Abu al-Darda' through Abu Muti' Mu'awiya ibn
Yahya from Artah ibn al-Mundhir from someone unnamed from Abu
al-Darda' by al-Tabarani, the rest being trustworthy, as stated by al-
Haythami in *Majma' al-Zawa'id* (10:60), Artah himself being highly
trustworthy, and Muti' fair as stated by al-Mundhiri in *al-Targhib*
(1997 ed. 4:32=1994 ed. 4:106 #4514). The hadith is further strengthened by Ibn 'Asakir's chain in *Ta'ziya al-Muslim* (p. 75) from Sa'id al-
Bajali from Shahr ibn Hawshab (cf. n. 202) from Abu al-Darda' and by
hadiths #23-26 and 32 below.
[153]Narrated from Abu Hurayra by Abu Ya'la in his *Musnad* and by al-
Tabarani in *al-Awsat*, al-Haythami in *Majma' al-Zawa'id* (10:60-61)
indicating that the former chain is sound but the latter weak because of
al-Walid ibn 'Abbad, who is unknown. However, he is also in Abu
Ya'la's chain and Ibn 'Adi in *al-Kamil* (7:84) stated that this hadith is
narrated only through him. The hadith is therefore weak with this chain
and wording – although confirmed by hadith #32 below – and mass-
transmitted with the wording "A party of my Community shall not

Al-Nawawi explained the term "the Hour" to mean "the spread of the wind [that shall take away the lives of the Believers]."[154]

15. The Prophet 🕌 said: "The anti-Christ shall come out into my Community and endure for forty days or months or years" – the narrator was unsure – "after which Allah 🕌 shall send 'Isa ibn Maryam 🕌, who looks exactly like 'Urwa ibn Mas'ud. 'Isa 🕌 shall pursue the anti-Christ and destroy him. Then people shall live for seven years without the least enmity among them. Then Allah 🕌 shall send a cool wind from the direction of *al-Shâm*, whereupon none shall remain on the face of the earth that has an atom's worth of goodness in their heart except they shall be taken away..."[155] The Prophet 🕌 described that wind as having "the scent of musk and the touch of silk."[156]

16. The Prophet 🕌 said: "O Allah, bless us in our *Shâm* and our Yemen!" They said: "O Messenger of Allah! and our Najd!" He did not reply but again said: "O Allah, bless us in our *Shâm* and our Yemen!" They said: "O Messenger of Allah! and our Najd!" He did not reply but again said: "O Allah, bless us in our *Shâm* and our Yemen!" They said: "O Messenger of Allah! and our Najd!" He said: "Thence shall come great upheavals and dissensions, and from it shall issue the side of the head of *Shaytân*."[157]

---

cease to remain victorious, standing for truth, until the Hour rises." See al-Kattani, *Nazm al-Mutanathir* (p. 141).

[154]In *Sharh Sahih Muslim* (1972 ed. 13:66).

[155]Narrated from 'Abd Allah ibn Àmr by Muslim and Ahmad as part of a longer hadith.

[156]Narrated from 'Uqba ibn 'Amir by Muslim.

[157]Narrated from Ibn 'Umar by al-Bukhari, al-Tirmidhi *(hasan sahîh gharîb)*, and Ahmad with three chains, one of which with the addition: "And in it [Najd] are nine tenths of all evil."

Al-Nawawi said: "Najd is the area that lies between Jurâsh (in Yemen) all the way to the rural outskirts of Kûfâ (in Iraq), and its Western border is the Hijaz. The author of *al-Matali'* said: Najd is all a province of al-Yamama."[158] Al-Fayruzabadi said: "Its geographical summit is Tihama and Yemen, its bottom is Iraq and *Shâm*, and it begins at Dhat 'Irqin [= Kufa][159] from the side of the Hijaz."[160] Al-Khattabi said: "Najd lies Eastward, and to those who are in Madina, their Najd is the desert of Iraq and its vicinities, which all lie East of the people of Madina. The original meaning of *najd* is 'elevated land' as opposed to *ghawr* which means declivity. Thus, Tihama is all part of al-Ghawr, and Mecca is part of Tihama."[161] This is confirmed by Ibn al-Athir's definition: "Najd is any elevated terrain, and it is a specific name for what lies outside the Hijaz and adjacent to Iraq."[162] Similarly Ibn Hajar stated: "Al-Dawudi said: 'Najd lies in the vicinity of Iraq.'"[163] Iraq itself lexicaly means river-shore or sea-shore, in reference to the Euphrates and the Tigris.[164]

All these explanations prove that those who say that Najd in the hadith denotes present-day Iraq exclusively of present-day Najd[165] are mistaken, as Najd at that time included not only Iraq but also – as in our present time – everything East of Madina, especially the regions South of Iraq. The proof for this is the hadith whereby the Prophet ﷺ pointed to Yemen and said: "Verily, belief is there; but hardness and coarseness of heart is with the blaring farmers *(al-faddadîn)*, the people of many

---

[158] Al-Nawawi in *Tahrir al-Tanbih* (p. 157, *s.v. "najd"*).
[159] As stated by Ibn Hajar in *Fath al-Bari* (1959 ed. 3:390).
[160] In *al-Qamus al-Muhit*, article *al-Najd*. See also *Mu'jam al-Buldan*.
[161] In Ibn Hajar, *Fath al-Bari* (1959 ed. 13:48).
[162] Ibn al-Athir, *al-Nihaya, s.v. n-j-d*.
[163] Ibn Hajar, *Fath al-Bari* (1959 ed. 13:48).
[164] Ibn al-Athir, *al-Nihaya, s.v. '-r-q*.
[165] Cf. al-Raba'i, *Fada'il al-Sham wa Dimashq* (p. 6, 27).

camels, where the two sides of the head of *Shaytân* shall appear, among [the tribes of] Rabi'a and Mudar."[166] Ibn Hajar identified these two tribes as "the most prestigious of the people of the East, the Quraysh – from which the Prophet ﷺ is issued – being a branch of Mudar."[167] This is confirmed by al-Bukhari's narration in seven places and Muslim's in six, from Ibn 'Umar, that the East *(al-Mashriq)* is the origin of dissension and the place where the side of the head of *Shaytân* would appear – or two sides in one narration of Muslim. The fact that Muslim narrated that Salim ibn 'Abd Allah ibn 'Umar applied this hadith to the people of Iraq does not limit its meaning to them. It only confirms that the Prophet ﷺ foresaw the dissension of the *Khawârij* among other dissensions hailing from the East, such as that of Musaylima the Liar and others.

Another proof is that the Prophet ﷺ had set Qarn al-Manazil as the starting-point *(mîqât)* for the state of consecration *(ihrâm)* for pilgrims coming from Najd, which in his time included Iraq. Later, the people of Iraq, finding Qarn al-Manazil too far out of the way for them, asked for something nearer, whereupon 'Umar ﷺ fixed Dhat 'Irqin as their *mîqât* as established in the following narrations:

a) "The Prophet ﷺ declared that the *ihrâm* of the people of Madina starts at Dhu al-Hulayfa; that of the people of *Shâm* starts at al-Juhfa; that of the people of Najd starts at Qarn al-Manazil; and that of the people of Yemen starts at Yalamlama."[168] Al-Nawawi said: "Qarn al-Manazil is the

---

[166]Narrated from Abu Mas'ud by al-Bukhari in three places and Muslim.
[167]Ibn Hajar, *Fath al-Bari* (1959 ed. 6:531).
[168]Narrated from Ibn 'Abbas by al-Bukhari and Muslim.

mountain of that name. Between it and Mecca on the East lies a distance of two legs of journey."[169]

b) "When these two cities were conquered – al-Basra and al-Kufa – they came to 'Umar ibn al-Khattab and said: 'O Commander of the Believers, Allah's Messenger gave Qarn as a limit to the people of Najd, and it is out of our way, so that if we want to go to Qarn it creates hardship for us.' 'Umar replied: 'See what lies nearest to it on your way.' So he determined Dhatu 'Irqin as a limit for them."[170] Ibn al-Athir said: "Ibn 'Abbas said: 'At Dhatu 'Irqin, facing Qarn,' Dhatu 'Irqin being the *mîqât* of the people of Iraq, and Qarn that of the people of Najd, and they are equidistant from the *Haram*."[171]

On the foregoing evidence one might make a case that Najd is synonymous with Iraq in the hadith in the general sense of the immediate East in relation to Madina. This view is supported by other narrations of the hadith "bless us in our *Shâm* and our Yemen" in which the terms "East" and "Iraq" are used interchangeably in the place of Najd:

a) The Prophet 🕮 said: "O Allah! Bless us in our *Shâm* and our Yemen!" A man said: "And our East, O Messenger of Allah!" The Prophet 🕮 repeated his invocation twice, and the man twice said: "And our East, O Messenger of Allah!" whereupon the Prophet 🕮 said: "Thence shall issue the side

---

[169]Al-Nawawi, *Tahrir al-Tanbih* (p. 157, *s.v. "qarn"*). Al-Shawkani in *Nayl al-Awtar* (4:295) said the same.
[170]Narrated from Ibn 'Umar by al-Bukhari.
[171]In *al-Nihaya s.v. h-dh-y.*

of the head of *Shaytân*. In it are nine tenths of disbelief. In it is the incurable disease *(al-dâ' al-'addâl)*."[172]

b) The Prophet 鑠 said: "O Allah! Bless us in our *sâ'* and in our *mudd* (i.e. in every measure)! Bless us in our Mecca and our Madina! Bless us in our *Shâm* and our Yemen!" A man said: "O Prophet of Allah, and our Iraq!" The Prophet 鑠 said: "In it is the side of the head of *Shaytân*. In it shall dissensions heave. Verily, disrespect *(al-jafâ')* lies in the East."[173]

17. The Prophet 鑠 said: "A huge fire shall issue from Hadramawt – or: from the direction of the sea of Hadramawt – before the Day of Resurrection, which shall cause a great movement of people." They said: "O Messenger of Allah! What do you order us to do at that time?" He said: "You must go to *Shâm*."[174]

18. The Prophet 鑠 said: "It shall reach the point when you will all be joining [opposite] armies: one army in *al-Shâm*, one in Yemen, and one in Iraq." 'Abd Allah ibn Hawala said:

---

[172]Narrated from Ibn 'Umar by al-Tabarani in *al-Awsat* (2:529 #1910) with a sound chain as indicated by al-Haythami in *Majma' al-Zawa'id* (3:305).

[173]Narrated from Ibn 'Abbas by al-Tabarani in *al-Kabir* (12:84 #12553) with a sound chain as indicated by al-Haythami in *Majma' al-Zawa'id* (3:305). Abu Nu'aym narrates something similar in the *Hilya* (1985 ed. 6:133).

[174]Narrated from Ibn 'Umar by al-Tirmidhi *(hasan gharîb sahîh)* who added that it is also narrated from Hudhayfa ibn Asid, Anas, Abu Hurayra, and Abu Dharr. Also narrated from Ibn 'Umar by Ahmad with five chains, Ibn Hibban in his *Sahih* (16:294) with a sound chain meeting al-Bukhari's criterion according to Shaykh Shu'ayb Arna'ut, Ibn Abi Shayba in his *Musannaf* (7:471), Ibn Tahman in his *Mashyakha* (#201), and Abu Ya'la in his *Musnad* (9:405) with a sound chain as stated by al-Haythami in *Majma' al-Zawa'id* (10:61).

"Choose for me, O Messenger of Allah! in case I live to see that day." The Prophet 鄒 said: "You must join *al-Shâm*, for it is Allah's chosen land in His earth. In it shall the chosen ones among His servants have protection. Otherwise, go to Yemen but be prepared to drink from still water. For Allah has given me a guarantee concerning *Shâm* and its people." 'Abd Allah ibn Hawala would add after narrating the above: "And whoever has Allah as his guarantor shall suffer no loss."[175] Another version states that some Companions said: "We are herdsmen, we cannot adapt to *Shâm*," whereby the Prophet 鄒 said: "Whoever cannot adapt to *Shâm*, let him go to Yemen. Verily, Allah has given me a guarantee concerning *Shâm*."[176]

19. In another version Ibn Hawala states: "When he noticed my dislike for *Shâm* he said: 'Do you know what Allah says about *Shâm*? Verily, Allah said: O *Shâm*, you are the quintessence *(safwa)* of My lands and I shall inhabit you

---

[175]Narrated from 'Abd Allah ibn Hawala by Abu Dawud and Ahmad with sound chains, Ibn Hibban in his *Sahih* (16:295), al-Hakim (4:510; 1990 ed. 4:555) who said it is *sahîh* and al-Dhahabi concurred, al-Tahawi in *Mushkil al-Athar* (2:35), al-Bayhaqi in *al-Sunan al-Kubra* (9:179), and Ibn 'Abd al-Salam in *Targhib Ahl al-Islam* (p. 15). Also narrated from Abu al-Darda' by al-Bazzar and al-Tabarani with a sound chain as indicated by al-Haythami in *Majma' al-Zawa'id* (10:58) after al-Mundhiri in *al-Targhib* (1997 ed. 4:30). Something similar is narrated from 'Abd Allah ibn Yazid by al-Tabarani with a very weak chain as indicated by al-Haythami in *Majma' al-Zawa'id* (10:58) and from Wathila ibn al-Asqa' by al-Tabarani in *al-Kabir* (22:55-58), specifying that those who were asking the Prophet 鄒 were Mu'adh and Hudhayfa. Al-Haythami in *Majma' al-Zawa'id* (10:59) stated that all al-Tabarani's chains of the latter narration were weak. Shaykh Ahmad al-Ghumari in *al-Mughir* (p. 71) declared this hadith forged by Mu'awiya's 鄒 supporters against 'Ali 鄒!

[176]Narrated from Abu al-Darda' by al-Bazzar and al-Tabarani with a sound chain as indicated by al-Haythami in *Majma' al-Zawa'id* (10:58).

with the chosen ones among My servants."[177] Ibn al-Athir defines *safw* and *safwa* in his dictionary *al-Nihaya* as "the best of any matter, its quintessence, and purest part."[178]

20. Related to the events mentioned by the Prophet 鏐 above is his hadith: "Strife shall take place after the death of a Caliph. A man of the people of Madina will come forth flying to Mecca. Some of the people of Mecca will come to him, bring him out against his will and swear allegiance to him between the Corner and the *Maqâm*. An expeditionary force will then be sent against him from *Shâm* but will be swallowed up in the desert between Mecca and Madina, and when the people see that, the Substitutes *(abdâl)* of *Shâm* and the best people of Iraq shall come to him and swear allegiance to him..."[179]

---

[177]Narrated by al-Tabarani with two chains of which one is fair according to al-Mundhiri in *al-Targhib* (1997 ed. 4:30). Something similar is narrated from al-'Irbad ibn Sariya by al-Tabarani in *al-Kabir* (18:251) with a sound chain according to al-Mundhiri in *al-Targhib* (1997 ed. 4:30) and al-Haythami in *Majma' al-Zawa'id* (10:58), chapter entitled *Fada'il al-Sham*, and from Ibn 'Umar by al-Tabarani and al-Bazzar with a weak chain according to al-Suyuti in *al-Durr al-Manthur*. Al-Suyuti also said that Ibn 'Asakir narrated it from Thabit ibn Ma'bad.

[178]The Prophet 鏐 also compared the world to a little rain water on a mountain plateau of which the *safw* had already been drunk and from which only the *kadar* or dregs remained. Narrated from Ibn Mas'ud by Ibn 'Asakir in *Tarikh Dimashq*. Al-Huwjiri and al-Qushayri mention it in their chapters on *tasawwuf* respectively in *Kashf al-Mahjub* and *al-Risala al-Qushayriyya*.

[179]Narrated from Umm Salama by Abu Dawud through three different good chains in his *Sunan*, Ahmad, Ibn Abi Shayba in his *Musannaf*, Abu Ya'la in his *Musnad* (12:369 #6940) with a fair chain according to Shaykh Husayn Asad, al-Tabarani in *al-Awsat* (2:89 #1175) and *al-Kabir* (23:389-390 #930-931), al-Hakim, Ibn Hibban in his *Sahih* (15:158-159 #6757) with a weak chain because of Muhammad ibn Yazid ibn Rufa'a – but he has been corroborated – and al-Bayhaqi.

21. The Prophet 鷹 said: "As I was sleeping I saw the Column of the Book being carried away from under my head. I feared lest it would be taken away, so I followed it with my eyes and saw that it was being planted in *al-Shâm*. Verily, belief in the time of dissensions will be in *al-Shâm*."[180] The Prophet repeated three times: "When the dissensions take place, belief shall be in *al-Shâm*." One version states: "Safety will be in *al-Shâm*."[181]

22. The Prophet 鷹 said: "I saw on the night that I was taken on a Night-Journey a white column resembling a pearl, which the angels were carrying. I said to them: 'What are you carrying?' They replied: 'The Column of the Book, we have been ordered to place it in *al-Shâm*.' Later, in my sleep, I saw that the Column of the Book was snatched away from under my headrest *(wisâdatî)*. I began to fear lest Allah the Almighty had abandoned the people of the earth. My eyes followed where it went. It was a brilliant light in front of me. Then I saw it was placed in *al-Shâm*." 'Abd Allah ibn Hawala said: "O Messenger of Allah, choose for me (where I should go)." The Prophet said: *'alayka bi al-shâm* – "You must go to *al-Shâm*."[182]

---

[180]Narrated from Abu al-Darda' by Ahmad with a chain whose narrators are all the men of the *sahih* and by al-Bazzar with a sound chain as indicated by al-Haythami in *Majma' al-Zawa'id* and al-Mundhiri in *al-Targhib* (1997 ed. 4:31). Also narrated by al-Tabarani in *al-Kabir* and *al-Awsat* and al-Hakim.

[181]Narrated from 'Abd Allah ibn 'Amr by al-Tabarani in *al-Kabir* and *al-Awsat*. Al-Haythami in *Majma' al-Zawa'id* (10:58) said the men in its chain are those of sound hadith except for Ibn Lahi'a (see n. 209).

[182]Narrated from Abu al-Darda' by al-Bazzar and from 'Abd Allah ibn Hawala by al-Tabarani in *al-Awsat*, both with sound chains as indicated by al-Haythami in *Majma' al-Zawa'id* (7:289, 10:58), and from 'Amr ibn al-'As by Ahmad with a weak chain according to al-Haythami (10:57).

23. The Prophet ﷺ said: "The rallying-place of Muslims on the day of Armageddon *(yawm al-malhama)* is in *al-Ghûta*, next to a city called Damascus *(Dimashq)*, which is among the best of the cities of *al-Shâm*." The narrator added in Abu Dawud: "Meaning in great battles."[183]

24. 'Abd Allah ibn 'Amr ibn al-'As narrated: "A time shall come when people shall see no believer remaining on earth except they have repaired to *Shâm*."[184] Ibn 'Abd al-Salam said of this report: "Such a statement is not made except by [Prophetic] prescription *(tawqîfan)*."[185] This is in conformity with the rules of hadith science, *tafsîr*, and *usûl* whereby news of the unseen in an authentic *mawqûf* Companion-report has the full force of a *marfû'* Prophetic narration.[186] The hadith master and imam of *Shâm* in his time al-Walid ibn Muslim (d. 195) reported that because of the Prophet's ﷺ insistence on the immense merits of *Shâm*, 10,000 eyes that had seen the Prophet ﷺ later entered *Shâm*.[187]

25. A similar Companion-report to that effect is that of Ka'b al-Ahbar[188] on the Prophet's ﷺ sovereignty over *Shâm* as part

---

[183]Narrated from Abu al-Darda' with sound chains by Abu Dawud, Ahmad, al-Mundhiri in *al-Tarhib wa al-Targhib* (4:63), and al-Hakim (4:486) who declared its chain sound while al-Dhahabi concurred. Also narrated from Makhul by Abu Dawud.

[184]Narrated by Ibn Abi Shayba in *al-Musannaf* (4:217) with a sound chain meeting Muslim's criterion, al-Hakim (4:457=1990 ed. 4:504) with a fair chain because of al-Husayn ibn Hafs who is *sadûq*, and Ibn al-Mubarak in *al-Jihad* (p. 152).

[185]Ibn 'Abd al-Salam, *Targhib Ahl al-Islam* (p. 24-25).

[186]See al-Qari's *Sharh Sharh Nukhba al-Fikar* (p. 548-549), al-Sakhawi's *Fath al-Mughith* (1:150-151), 'Itr, *Manhaj al-Naqd* (p. 328).

[187]In Ibn 'Abd al-Salam, *Targhib Ahl al-Islam* (p. 25).

[188]This trustworthy *Tâbi'î* is *mukhadram* i.e. he may have met the Prophet ﷺ and is therefore accorded the same respect as the

of his qualities mentioned in the Torah according to Allah's saying ⟨**Those who follow the messenger, the unlettered Prophet, whom they can find described in the Torah and the Gospel (which are) with them**⟩ (7:157):

* Ibn 'Abbas asked Ka'b al-Ahbar: "What qualities of Allah's Messenger 鐌 do you find written in the Torah?" Ka'b replied: "We find him named Muhammad ibn 'Abd Allah, his birthplace Mecca, his place of migration Tâbah [=Madina], and his kingdom *Shâm*. He is not coarse of speech nor boisterous in the market-places. He does not return wrong with wrong but forgives and pardons."[189] In another version Ka'b adds: "His Community are the Praisers *(al-hammâdûn)*. They praise Allah in every happy and sad occasion, and extol Allah on every height. They cleanse their limbs, wear the waist-wrap, and line up for their prayers just as they do for battle. The sound they make in their places of worship is like that of bees. Their callers [to prayer] can be heard in the air of the heaven."[190]

Companions. Even if he is known to relate Israelite reports *(isrâ'îliyyât)*, these reports are accepted when they are confirmed by the Qur'an and/or Sunna. This rule is spelled out by the Prophet 鐌 in his saying: "Convey [the Religion] on my behalf, even a single verse, and narrate without constraint *(haraj)* from the Israelites, but whoever purposely tells a lie about me, let him prepare himself for his seat in the Fire." Narrated from 'Abd Allah ibn 'Amr ibn al-'As by al-Bukhari, al-Tirmidhi *(hasan sahîh)*, Ahmad, and al-Darimi. Al-Shafi'i said: "It means: narrate from the Israelites whatever you know not to be a lie, and whatever you consider to be possible *(mâ tujawwizûnahu)*, there is no contraint on you not to narrate it from them." In Ibn Hajar, *Fath al-Bari* (1959 ed. 6:498).
[189]Narrated by Ibn Sa'd in his *Tabaqat* (1:360) with a strong chain except that Mu'awiya ibn Salih's shaykh, Abu Farwa, is unknown.
[190]Narrated by al-Darimi in his *Sunan* with a sound chain except for Abu Farwa, who is unknown. The only person to narrate from him in the Nine Books is Mu'awiya ibn Salih ibn Hudayr, who is trustworthy

- In another version Ka'b said: "The description of Muhammad ﷺ in the Torah is as follows: 'Muhammad is My chosen servant. He is neither rough nor harsh. He is not boisterous in the market-places nor does he return wrong with wrong, but he forgives and pardons. His birthplace is Mecca, his place of migration is Madina, and his kingdom is *Shâm*.'"[191]

- In another version Ka'b said: "In the first line [of the Torah's text] is: 'Muhammad the Messenger of Allah, My elect servant. He is neither rough nor harsh. He is not boisterous in the market-places nor does he return wrong with wrong, but he forgives and pardons. His birthplace is Mecca, his place of migration is Madina, and his kingdom is *Shâm*.' In the second line is: 'Muhammad the Messenger of Allah. His Community are the Praisers. They praise Allah in every happy and sad occasion. They praise Allah in every place and extol Him on every high place. They observe the movements of the sun and accomplish the prayer when its time comes, even if they find themselves on top of a refuse-heap. They wear the waist-wrap and cleanse their limbs. The sound of their voices in the night air is like that of bees.'"[192]

(thiqa) as stated in Arna'ut and Ma'ruf, *Tahrir al-Taqrib* (3:394 #6762).
[191] Narrated by Ibn Sa'd in his *Tabaqat* (1:360) with a strong chain except that Mu'awiya ibn Salih does not name the link between him and Ka'b, which is probably Abu Farwa, who is unknown.
[192] Narrated by Ibn 'Asakir in *Tarikh Dimashq* (1:175-176) and al-Darimi with a very weak chain because of al-Darimi's shaykh, Zayd ibn 'Awf, who is discarded as a narrator. Ibn 'Abd al-Salam cites this report in *Targhib Ahl al-Islam* (p. 25-26).

- There are other similar strong reports from Ka'b that do not mention Mecca, Madina, and *Shâm*.[193]

- 'Abd Allah ibn 'Amr ibn al-'As, 'Abd Allah ibn Salam, 'A'isha, and Wahb ibn Munabbih all relate something similar to the above reports but without mention of Mecca, Madina, and *Shâm*.[194]

26. The Prophet ﷺ was also related to say: "The fortress *(ma'qal)* of the Muslims against the great battles shall be in Damascus, their fortress against the anti-Christ shall be *Bayt al-Maqdis*, and their fortress against Gog and Magog *(Ya'jûj wa Ma'jûj)* shall be *Bayt al-Tûr*."[195] Related to these two narrations are Abu Dawud's reports from the *Tâbi'în* whereby "The Byzantines shall cut through *al-Shâm* for forty days, and none but Damascus and Amman shall repel them"[196] and "One of the foreign kings shall dominate all the cities except Damascus."[197]

---

[193]Narrated from Ka'b by al-Tabari in his *Tafsir* (9:83), Ibn Sa'd in *al-Tabaqat al-Kubra* (1:360), al-Bayhaqi in his *Dala'il al-Nubuwwa*, and Abu Nu'aym in his.

[194]'Abd Allah ibn 'Amr: Narrated by Ahmad in his *Musnad*, al-Tabari in his *Tafsir* (9:83), al-Bukhari in *al-Adab al-Mufrad* (p. 95), al-Bayhaqi in *Dala'il al-Nubuwwa*, Ibn Kathir in his *Tafsir* (1:421), al-Qurtubi in his (7:299), and al-Shawkani in his (2:254); 'Abd Allah ibn Salam: Ibn Sa'd in *al-Tabaqat al-Kubra* (1:360); 'A'isha: *ibid.* (1:363), al-Hakim (1990 ed. 2:671) who declared it *sahîh*, and al-Bayhaqi and Abu Nu'aym in *Dala'il al-Nubuwwa*; Wahb: Narrated by Ibn Abi Hatim in his *Tafsir* and Abu Nu'aym in *Dala'il al-Nubuwwa* as cited by al-Suyuti in *al-Durr al-Manthur* for verse 7:157.

[195]Narrated *mursal* from the *Tâbi'î* Abu al-Zahiriyya Hudayr ibn Kurayb by Ibn Abi Shayba in his *Musannaf* (4:217, 6:409), and Abu al-Zahiriyya is trustworthy *(thiqa)* as stated in Arna'ut and Ma'ruf's *Tahrir al-Taqrib* (1:256 #1153).

[196]Narrated from Makhul by Abu Dawud with a sound chain.

[197]Narrated from Abu al-A'yas 'Abd al-Rahman ibn Salman by Abu Dawud with a fair chain.

27. The Prophet 🕮 said: "When the great battles take place, an army of foreigners *(al-mawâlî)* shall come out of Damascus, the noblest of the Arabs in knightship and most skillful in weaponry. Through them shall Allah support the Religion."[198]

28. The Prophet 🕮 said: "The place of the Final Gathering is *al-Shâm.*" *(Al-Shâm ardu al-mahshar.)* [199] Another version says: "The place of the Final Gathering and Resurrection is *al-Shâm.*" *(Al-Shâm ardu al-mahshar wa al-manshar.)* [200] Al-Qari said that the letter of this report means that *al-Shâm* is the starting-point for these events or that it shall be expanded so as to contain all humankind.[201]

---

[198]Narrated from Abu Hurayra by al-Tabarani in *Musnad al-Shamiyyin* (2:414), al-Hakim (4:548=1990 ed. 4:591) who said its chain is sound and al-Dhahabi concurred, and Ibn Majah – the latter without mention of Damascus – but al-Busiri in *Misbah al-Zujaja* (4:206) avered that the chain is only fair *(hasan)* because of 'Uthman ibn Abi al-'Atika. However, the latter is weak for uncorroborated reports according to Arna'ut and Ma'ruf in *al-Tahrir* (2:439 #4483), and so the narration is weak.

[199]Narrated from Ibn 'Abbas by al-Bazzar, Ibn al-Mundhir, Ibn Abi Hatim, Ibn Mardawayh, al-Bayhaqi in *al-Ba'th* as well as *Shu'ab al-Iman* (1:316) but the latter without chain, and Ibn 'Uyayna in his *Tafsir* as cited by Ibn Hajar in *Fath al-Bari* (1959 ed. 11:380); and from 'Abd al-Rahman ibn Ghanm – with a chain questioned by Ibn Kathir in his *Tafsir* (verses 17:76-77) – by Ibn Abi Hatim, al-Bayhaqi in *al-Dala'il*, and Ibn 'Asakir. Cf. Ibn Hajar, *Fath al-Bari* (1959 ed. 8:111-112) on Tabuk.

[200]Narrated from Maymuna bint Sa'd by Ahmad and Ibn Majah with a sound chain as stated by al-Busiri in his *Zawa'id* (2:14) and al-Nawawi in *al-Majmu'* and from Abu Dharr by Ibn Marduyah, Ibn 'Asakir, and Abu al-Hasan ibn Shuja' al-Raba'i in *Fada'il al-Sham* with a fair chain according to al-Suyuti in *al-Jami' al-Saghir* and al-'Ajluni in *Kashf al-Khafa'*.

[201]In al-Mubarakfuri, *Tuhfa al-Ahwadhi* (6:345) and 'Azim Abadi, *'Awn al-Ma'bud* (11:289).

29. Asma' Bint Yazid narrated that Abu Dharr (al-Ghifari) used to serve the Prophet 攤 and when he finished he would go to the mosque and sleep. The mosque was his house. One time the Prophet 攤 came in and found Abu Dharr lying on the ground. He nudged him with his foot and Abu Dharr sat up. The Prophet 攤 said: "Sleeping?" He replied: "O Messenger of Allah, where else can I sleep? I have no house other than this." The Prophet 攤 said: "What will you do if they expel you from it?" He said: "I will repair to *al-Shâm*, for verily *al-Shâm* is the land of emigration, the land of the Final Gathering, and the land of Prophets. So I shall be one of its dwellers." The Prophet 攤 said: "What will you do if they expel you from *al-Shâm*?" He said: "I will come back here and make it my house and my dwelling." The Prophet 攤 said: "What if they expel you from it a second time?" He replied: "Then I will take up my sword and fight them off until I die." The Prophet 攤 looked displeased and he held him firmly and said: "Shall I tell you of a better way?" He said: "Yes, may my father and mother be ransomed for you, O Messenger of Allah!" The Prophet 攤 said: "Let them lead you whither they lead you, and let yourself be taken whither they take you, until you meet me again in that very state."[202]

30. Shurayh ibn 'Ubayd said that the people of *al-Shâm* were mentioned in front of 'Ali ibn Abi Talib while he was in Iraq, and some people said to him: "Curse them, O

---

[202]Ahmad narrated it with a weak chain because of Shahr ibn Hawshab al-Ash'ari al-Shami as per al-Haythami in *Majma' al-Zawa'id* (5:222-223) and al-Arna'ut and Ma'ruf in *al-Tahrir* (2:122 #2830), although Ibn Hajar in *Fath al-Bari* (1989 ed. 3:65) and al-Dhahabi declared him reliable after the opinion of several of the early Imams. Nevertheless, the hadith is authentic with regard to Abu Dharr's words regarding *al-Shâm* as they are authentically reported from the Prophet 攤 himself as established in the previous hadith.

Commander of the Believers." He replied: No, I heard the
Messenger of Allah 鑅 say: "The Substitutes *(al-Abdâl)* are
in *al-Shâm* and they are forty men, every time one of them
dies, Allah substitutes another in his place.[203] By means of
them Allah brings down the rain, gives us victory over our

---

[203] Al-Suyuti in *al-Ta'aqqubat 'ala al-Mawdu'at* asserted that the
Prophetic report of the existence of the *Abdâl* is *sahîh* and its general
meaning is *mutawâtir*. This is confirmed by the hadith master al-
Kattani in his *Nazm al-Mutanathir* (p. 220-221). Ibn Hajar said as
reported by al-Munawi in *Fayd al-Qadir*: "Some of the reports on the
Abdâl are sound, some weak." The claims of Ibn al-Qayyim in *al-
Manar al-Munif* (p. 136) that all the Prophetic reports that mention the
Abdâl are invalid and that of his teacher Ibn Taymiyya whereby "the
name of *Abdâl* does not appear in a single hadith whether sound or
weak" are attributed to stubbornness and fanaticism by al-Munawi in
Fayd al-Qadir. Al-Suyuti's position is supported by the fact that the
Salaf believed in the existence of the *Abdâl*, and Ibn Taymiyya himself
included such belief into his Islamic creed entitled *al-'Aqida al-
Wasitiyya*!

Al-Sakhawi cited Shurayh ibn 'Ubayd's narration as the
strongest report on the *Abdâl* and said in *al-Maqasid al-Hasana* (p. 33
#8): "What makes this hadith stronger and indicates its currency among
the Imams is the statement of our Imam, al-Shafi'i, concerning a
certain man: 'We considered him one of the *Abdâl*' and al-Bukhari's
words concerning another: 'They did not doubt that he was one of the
Abdâl,' and other than these two among the highly meticulous scholars,
hadith masters, and imams [such as Qatada, see above] also used this
description for other people, stating that they were of the *Abdâl*." Abu
Hatim said of 'Abd al-Kabir ibn Mu'afi that he was considered one of
the *Abdâl*. Abu Dawud in the *Sunan* narrates the same from
Muhammad ibn 'Isa about 'Anbasa al-Qurashi. Ibn Majah in his *Sunan*
states the same of Yahya ibn 'Uthman al-Himsi, al-Khatib in *al-Jami'
li Akhlaq al-Rawi* (2:229) of Abu 'Umar al-Khawlani, al-Bayhaqi in
the *Shu'ab* (4:137) of Jabir ibn Marzuq, al-Daraqutni in *al-'Ilal* (6:63)
of al-Nadr ibn Kathir al-Sa'di, al-Nawawi in *Bustan al-'Arifin* (p. 31)
of the hadith master Hammad ibn Salama ibn Dinar (d. 167), al-Fattani
in his *Tadhkira* of Hubaysh ibn Dinar, etc.

enemies, and averts punishment from the people of *al-Shâm*."[204]

---

[204]Narrated by Ahmad in his *Musnad* and *Fada'il al-Sahaba* (2:906) with a sound chain as indicated by al-Sakhawi in *al-Maqasid*, al-Haythami in *Majma' al-Zawa'id*, al-Munawi in *Fayd al-Qadir*, al-Suyuti in *al-Khabar al-Dall*, and al-Ghumari in his notes on the latter who all declared its narrators trustworthy. Al-Suyuti similarly declared it sound in *al-Jami' al-Saghir*. Al-Maqdisi in *al-Mukhtara* (2:110) cites the same chain while Ibn 'Asakir in his *Tarikh* narrates it through Isma'il ibn 'Iyash from Safwan ibn 'Umar al-Saksaki from Shurayh from 'Ali from the Prophet ﷺ as in al-Suyuti's *al-Khabar al-Dall* (p. 4). To the correct objection that the chain is *munqati'* because Shurayh never met 'Ali ﵁ al-Haythami (10:62) replied: "Shurayh narrated from al-Miqdad [ibn al-Aswad], who is older than 'Ali." Al-Suyuti in *al-Khabar al-Dall* (p. 4-5) cites Ibn 'Asakir's narration of corroborating chains of the same hadith from 'Abd Allah ibn Zurayr al-Ghafili from 'Ali from the Prophet ﷺ with weak or very weak chains.

Al-Sakhawi mentions Shurayh's narration in his *Maqasid* (p. 33 #8) and states that it is more likely a saying of 'Ali himself. This is confirmed by:

- The *mawqûf* narration of the same hadith from 'Abd Allah ibn Zurayr from 'Ali in Ibn Yunus's *Tarikh Misr* as cited by Suyuti in *al-Khabar al-Dall* (p. 5-6);
- The sound *mawqûf* narration of the same hadith from 'Abd Allah ibn Zurayr from 'Ali with a similar chain through 'Uthman ibn Sa'id al-Darimi by al-Hakim (1990 ed. 4:596) who said it is *sahîh*, and al-Dhahabi concurred;
- The sound *mawqûf* narration of the same hadith from al-Zuhri from 'Abd Allah ibn Safwan from 'Ali in Imam Ahmad's *Fada'il al-Sahaba* (2:905), al-Azdi's *al-Jami'* (11:249), Ibn Abi al-Dunya's *al-Awliya'* (p. 30), al-Bayhaqi, al-Khallal's *al-Awliya'*, al-Maqdisi in two places in *al-Mukhtara* (2:111-112), and Ibn 'Asakir.
- The same *mawqûf* report is also narrated from al-Zuhri from Safwan ibn 'Abd Allah ibn Safwan from Shurayh from 'Ali by Ibn Rahuyah, al-Dhahabi in *'Ilal Hadith al-Zuhri*, and al-Bayhaqi in *Dala'il al-Nubuwwa*, and al-Suyuti cited many other chains.

Even if the report were established as sound only from 'Ali, it would still have the force of a Prophetic narration as it contains

The Prophet ﷺ said: "The earth will never lack forty men similar to the Friend of the Merciful [Ibrahim ﷺ], and through them people receive rain and are given help. None of them dies except Allah substitutes another in his place." Qatada said: "We do not doubt that al-Hasan is one of them."[205]

In another narration the Prophet ﷺ said: "The Substitutes in this Community are thirty like Ibrahim the Friend of the Merciful. Every time one of them dies, Allah substitutes another one in his place."[206]

Another version adds: "By means of them the world turns (bihim taqûm al-ard), you receive rain, and you achieve victory."[207]

---

information about the unseen which is not subject to opinion, and is confirmed by other narrations.

[205]Narrated from Anas by al-Tabarani in al-Awsat with a fair chain and from Ibn Mas'ud with a chain containing two unknown narrators, both as stated in Majma' al-Zawa'id (10:63). Ibn Hibban narrates it in al-Tarikh through Abu Hurayra as: "The earth will never lack thirty men similar to Ibrahim ﷺ the Friend of the Merciful, and through whom you are helped, receive your sustenance, and receive rain." The latter is unanimously a forged narration as stated by Ibn al-Jawzi in al-Mawdu'at, Ibn Hibban in al-Tarikh, al-Suyuti in al-Ta'aqqubat, al-Munawi in Fayd al-Qadir, and al-Fattani in his Tadhkira.

[206]Narrated from 'Ubada ibn al-Samit by Ahmad in his Musnad, al-Hakim al-Tirmidhi in Nawadir al-Usul, Ibn Marduyah, Ibn Kathir in his Tafsir for the verse ﴾And if Allah had not repelled some men by others the earth would have been corrupted﴿ (2:251), and al-Khallal in Karamat al-Awliya'. Al-Haythami in Majma' al-Zawa'id (10:62) indicated that Ahmad's chain was sound, but Ahmad himself declared the hadith "condemned" (munkar) after narrating it. However, al-Suyuti declared it sahîh in al-Jami' al-Saghir.

[207]Al-Tabarani in al-Kabir and al-Bazzar from 'Ubada ibn al-Samit. Al-Suyuti declared it sahîh in al-Jami' al-Saghir and al-Munawi did

A similar narration of Ibn 'Abbas states: "The world after Nuh ﷾ has never been without seven people through which Allah ﷻ wards off evil from humankind."[208]

31. The Prophet ﷺ said: "Do not curse the people of *Shâm* but curse their worse men. For among them are the *Abdâl*."[209]

In another version 'Awf ibn Malik said to the people of Egypt: "Do not curse the people of *Shâm*, for I heard Allah's Messenger ﷺ say: 'Among them are the *Abdâl*. Through them you achieve victory and receive sustenance."[210]

Another version states that 'Ali ibn Abi Talib said to the people of Iraq: "Do not curse the people of *Shâm*, for among

---

not contradict him in *Fayd al-Qadir*. However, al-Haythami in *Majma' al-Zawa'id* (10:63) said that their chains contains two unknown narrators, which makes the narration weak. Al-Tabarani in *al-Kabir* (10:181) also narrates from Ibn Mas'ud a similar narration mentioning the number forty.

[208] Narrated by Ahmad in *al-Zuhd* and al-Khallal in *Karamat al-Awliya'* with a sound chain according to al-Suyuti in *al-Durr al-Manthur*.

[209] Narrated as part of a longer hadith from 'Ali by al-Tabarani in *al-Awsat* with a chain of trustworthy narrators except for 'Abd Allah ibn Lahi'a, and he is fair *(hasan)* as stated by Ibn 'Adi in *al-Kamil* (4:144 #977, 4:153): "Ibn Lahi'a's narrations are fair, the *Salaf* did not declare him weak, and he is fair as a narrator." Moreover, he relates this narration from 'Iyash ibn 'Abbas, 'Abd Allah ibn Hubayra, and al-Harith ibn Yazid.

[210] Narrated by al-Tabarani in *al-Kabir* (18:65) with a chain containing 'Amr ibn Waqid who is discarded as a narrator as stated in *al-Taqrib*, and Shahr ibn Hawshab who is weak (see n. 202). Al-Suyuti declared it *hasan* in *al-Jami' al-Saghir*, and al-Munawi did not contradict him in *Fayd al-Qadir*, but this is incorrect as the chain is very weak.

them are the Substitutes *(al-Abdâl)*, but curse their injustice."[211]

Wahb ibn Munabbih said: I saw the Prophet ﷺ in my sleep and said: "O Messenger of Allah! Where are the Substitutes *(budalâ')* of your Community?" He gestured with his hand towards *Shâm*. I said: "O Messenger of Allah! Are there not any in Iraq?" He said: "Yes: Muhammad ibn Wasi', Hassan ibn Abi Sinan, and Malik ibn Dinar who walks among the people just like Abu Dharr in his time."[212]

32. The Prophet ﷺ said: "When the people of *Shâm* become corrupt, no goodness shall be left among you. There shall not cease to be a group in my Community that shall remain victorious over all people; those who betray or desert them cannot harm them in the least; and so until the Hour rises."[213] Al-Tirmidhi narrated from al-Bukhari that 'Ali ibn al-Madini said: "These are the hadith authorities *(ashâb al-hadîth)*." Al-Mubarakfuri explained the phrase "there shall be no goodness left among you" as meaning "for residing in *Shâm* or going there."[214]

---

[211]Narrated by al-Hakim who graded it sound *(sahîh)*, and al-Dhahabi concurred.

[212]Narrated from Julays by Ahmad in *al-Zuhd*, Ibn Abi al-Dunya, Abu Nu'aym, al-Bayhaqi, and Ibn 'Asakir.

[213]Narrated from Qurra ibn Iyas by al-Tirmidhi *(hasan sahîh)*, Ahmad with three sound chains, and Abu Dawud al-Tayalisi in his *Musnad* (2:145 #1076); also Ibn Hibban in his *Sahih* (16:292-293 #7302-7303) with two sound chains according to Shaykh Shu'ayb Arna'ut, al-Tabarani in *al-Kabir* (19:27), Abu Nu'aym in *Hilya al-Awliya'* (1985 ed. 7:230-231), and al-Khatib in *Tarikh Baghdad* (8:417, 10:182), the last four without the second part. The first part is mass-narrated *(mutawâtir)* as pointed out elsewhere. Al-Tirmidhi added that it is also narrated from 'Abd Allah ibn Hawala, Ibn 'Umar, Zayd ibn Thabit, and 'Abd Allah ibn 'Amr.

[214]In *Tuhfa al-Ahwadhi* (6:359).

33. Another version states that the Prophet ﷺ said: "Goodness is ten parts, nine in *al-Shâm* and one in the remaining countries; and evil is ten parts, one in *al-Shâm* and nine in the remaining countries. When the people of *Shâm* become corrupt, no goodness shall be left in you."[215] Another version attributes this hadith to Ibn Mas'ud.[216] Ka'b al-Ahbar said: "There will still be time for people until the head is struck. When the head is struck they shall perish." He was asked: "What is the striking of the head?" He replied: "The destruction of *Shâm*."[217]

34. The Prophet ﷺ is related to say: "The world shall be destroyed forty years before *Shâm* is." *(Tukhrabu al-ardu qabla al-Shâmi bi arba'îna sana.)*[218] Nu'aym ibn Hammad al-Marwazi (d. 288) narrates it *mawqûf* from Ka'b al-Ahbar and Abu al-Zahiriyya.[219] He also narrates:

---

[215]Narrated from 'Abd Allah ibn 'Amr by al-Khatib in *al-Muttafaq wa al-Muftaraq* and Ibn 'Asakir in *Tarikh Dimashq* (1:143) with a fair chain because of al-Wadîn ibn 'Ata' who is *sadûq hasan al-hadîth* as stated by Arna'ut and Ma'ruf in *al-Tahrir* (4:59-60 #7408). Ibn 'Abd al-Salam cites it in *Targhib Ahl al-Islam* (p. 22-23) and Yaqut in *Mu'jam al-Buldan* (3:312).
[216]Narrated *mawqûf* from Ibn Mas'ud by al-Hakim (4:505=1990 ed. 4:550) who said its chain is sound and al-Dhahabi concurred, al-Tabarani in *al-Kabir* (9:177), and Ahmad in *Fada'il al-Sahaba* (2:897-898), the latter two with chains containing 'Abd Allah ibn Dirar who is weak as stated by al-Haythami in *Majma' al-Zawa'id* (10:60), and Ibn 'Asakir.
[217]Narrated from Abu al-Nadr by Nu'aym ibn Hammad in *Kitab al-Fitan* (1:237).
[218]Narrated from 'Awf ibn Malik by Ibn 'Asakir in *Tarikh Dimashq* (1:185) and thus cited by Ibn 'Abd al-Salam in *Targhib Ahl al-Islam* (p. 23).
[219]Nu'aym ibn Hammad, *Kitab al-Fitan* (1:237, 1:254).

- from Ka'b: "In the huge final battle *(al-malhama al-'uzmâ)*, the coasts of *Shâm* shall be destroyed until the coasts weep over their destruction along wih the other cities and towns."[220]

- from 'Abd Allah ibn 'Amr: "There shall be in *Shâm* a dissension *(fitna)* in which all sorts of briberies *(rushâ)* and evils *(ashrâr)* shall rise. The foolish and the lowborn among them shall be many. It shall reach the point when they shall worship their leaders in the same way that they used to before [Islam]."[221]

35. Another hadith of the Prophet ﷺ states: "The people of the West *(ahl al-gharb)* shall not cease to be victorious, standing for truth, until the Hour rises."[222] Al-Nawawi said:

> Ibn al-Madini said that [it is read *al-gharab* so that] "the people of *al-gharab*" are the Arabs and '*al-gharab*' refers to the very large pail *(al-dalaw)*, as they are known to use it. Others said that *al-gharb* denotes the West of the earth. Mu'adh ibn Jabal said: "It is *Shâm*."[223] Another narration says *Bayt al-Maqdis*.[224] It is also said that it

---

[220]Nu'aym ibn Hammad, *Kitab al-Fitan* (2:500).
[221]Nu'aym ibn Hammad, *Kitab al-Fitan* (1:237).
[222]Narrated from Sa'd ibn Abi Waqqas by Muslim, Abu Ya'la in his *Musnad* (2:118) with a sound chain according to Shaykh Husayn Asad, and al-Tabarani in *al-Awsat*.
[223]After the hadith of Mu'awiya narrated by Ahmad with a fair chain and Bukhari in his *Sahih*: "A party of my Community shall remain in charge of Allah's Order, unharmed by those who betray or desert or oppose them, until the coming of Allah's order while they are victorious over all people." Malik ibn Yakhamir al-Saksaki stood up and said: "O Commander of the Believers! I heard Mu'adh ibn Jabal say: 'They are the people of al-Shâm.'"
[224]Narrated from Abu Umama by Ahmad and al-Tabarani in *al-Awsat* as cited in *Fath al-Bari* (1959 ed. 13:295).

refers to the people of *Shâm* and whatever lies beyond it. Al-Qadi 'Iyad said: "It is said that *ahl al-gharb* denotes the people of hardship and long-suffering, as the *gharb* of anything is its utmost *(hadd).*"[225]

Al-Qurtubi said:

The beginning of the West in relation to the Prophet's صلى الله عليه وسلم city is *al-Shâm* and its end the continental far-Western tip of the earth, all that lies in between being 'the Occident' *(al-maghrib)*. So then, is what is meant by *ahl al-gharb*, the entire West, or its beginning? Both are possible. Abu Bakr al-Turtushi said in an epistle he sent to the farthest part of Morocco: "Allah knows best whether the Prophet صلى الله عليه وسلم meant you by this hadith or whether he meant the people of North Africa and Andalusia *(ahl al-maghrib)* as a whole, because of their staunch adherence to the Sunna and the Congregation, their exemption from innovations in the Religion, and their strict following in the steps of the pious *Salaf.*"[226]

Ibn Abi Hujja said:

It refers to the wise scholars of knowledge *(al-'ulamâ')*, as *al-ghar(a)b* homonymously denotes a huge pail, or the place where the sun sets, or the abundant shedding of tears. Therefore, the meaning of "the people of *al-gharb* shall not cease" etc. is: the people that shed tears of humble Godwariness knowing Allah and His rulings, shall not cease to be victorious.

Al-Qurtubi cited the preceding paragraph and commented:

---

[225] Al-Nawawi, *Sharh Sahih Muslim* (1972 ed. 13:68).
[226] In al-Suyuti, *al-Dibaj 'ala Sahih Muslim* (4:514).

This interpretation is confirmed by the Prophet's 襲 hadith: "He for whom Allah desires great good, He grants him understanding in the Religion. There shall not cease to be among the Muslims a party who shall fight on the side of truth and remain victorious over those who oppose them until the Day of Resurrection."[227] The latter narration literally ties the first part with the last. Allah knows best.[228]

Al-Suyuti said:

What supports the view that by *gharb* is meant the West of the earth is the narration of 'Abd ibn Humayd and Baqiy ibn Makhlad[229] with the wording: "The people of the West *(ahl al-gharb)* shall not cease to be victorious"[230] and al-Daraqutni's narration: "A party in my Community shall not cease to be victorious, standing for truth in the

---

[227]Narrated from Mu'awiya by Muslim in his *Sahih*. There are variant versions for this mass-narrated hadith as stated by al-Kattani in *Nazm al-Mutanathir*.

[228]Al-Qurtubi, *Tafsir*, verse ❴Of every troop of them, a party only should go forth, that they (who are left behind) may gain sound knowledge in religion, and that they may warn their folk when they return to them, so that they may beware❵ (9:122).

[229]Baqiy ibn Makhlad ibn Yazid, Abu 'Abd al-Rahman al-Qurtubi al-Andalusi, the pious ascetic and worshipful hadith master and student of Yahya ibn Yahya al-Laythi, he compiled a *Tafsir* and a *Musnad* in which he narrated from 1,300 Companions according to *fiqh* sub-headings.

[230]I could not find such a narration in 'Abd ibn Humayd's *Musnad* and his narration (p. 115) from Mu'awiya states: "O people of *Shâm*! Al-Ansari [Zayd ibn Arqam] narrated to me that the Prophet 襲 said: 'A party in my Community shall not cease to stand for truth until the coming of Allah's Order,' and verily I consider that that party is you, O people of *Shâm*!"

Occident *(fi al-maghrib)* until the Hour rises."[231] Nor would it be far-fetched to say that by Occident, Egypt is meant, for it is included by all among the Western parts.[232]

Ibn Hajar said:

It was also said that by *ahl al-gharb* are meant the people of strength and striving in *jihâd*.... It is possible to put together the reports and say that the people to which they refer shall be in *Bayt al-Maqdis*, which is part of *Shâm*, use the pail for watering, and possess fighting-strength against the enemy as well as zeal and intensity.[233]

Nearly all these meanings were cited for *ahl al-gharb* by the lexicographers.[234]

36. The Prophet ﷺ said: "'Isa ibn Maryam عليه السلام shall descend at the White Minaret East of Damascus, wearing two lightly-saffroned garments resting his hands upon the wings of two angels. Whenever he moves his head it trickles water, and when he raises it, the like of pearl droplets fall from it."[235]

---

[231] I could not find such a narration in al-Daraqutni's *Sunan* or *'Ilal*, and the narration from al-Mughira in the latter (7:128) states "A party in my Community shall not cease to be victorious, standing for truth, until the coming of Allah's Order" without mention of the words "in the Occident."

[232] Al-Suyuti, *al-Dibaj 'ala Sahih Muslim* (4:514).

[233] Ibn Hajar, *Fath al-Bari* (1959 ed. 13:295).

[234] Cf. Al-Fayruzabadi in *al-Qamus al-Muhit*, Ibn al-Athir in *al-Nihaya*, and Ibn Manzur in *Lisan al-'Arab*.

[235] Narrated from al-Nawwas ibn Sam'an al-Kilabi as part of a long hadith by Muslim, al-Tirmidhi *(hasan sahih gharîb)*, Ibn Majah, and Ahmad; also by Abu Dawud with a sound chain and al-Hakim who said it is *sahîh* – al-Dhahabi concurred; and from Aws ibn Aws al-Thaqafi by al-Tabarani in *al-Kabir* (1:186, 19:196) with a sound chain as indicated by al-Haythami in *Majma' al-Zawa'id* (8:205).

37. The Prophet ﷺ said: "There shall be successive emigrations *(hijra ba'da hijra)*, at which time the best of human beings shall rally to Ibrahim's ﷺ haven *(muhâjar)*. Only the most evil of people shall remain on the earth. Their own abodes shall loathe them, Allah Himself shall detest them, and Hellfire shall collect them together with apes and swine."[236] "Ibrahim's haven" is *al-Shâm*.[237]

38. A hadith narration states that the Prophet ﷺ said: "*Shâm* is the quintessence of Allah's lands. There do the quintessence of his servants go for protection. Therefore, whoever departs from *Shâm* to go somewhere else earns [Allah's] anger *(sakhta)*, and whoever enters it from somewhere else earn His mercy."[238]

39. Another narration states that the Prophet ﷺ said: "The quintessence of Allah's lands is *Shâm*. In it are the quintessence of His creatures and servants. Verily, a vast number *(thulla)*

---

[236]Narrated from 'Abd Allah ibn 'Amr by Abu Dawud and Ahmad with weak chains because of Shahr ibn Hawshab (see n. 202), but the hadith is also narrated from Abu Hurayra by al-Hakim (1:510) with a chain he declared *sahîh*, and Dhahabi concurred; however, the latter's chain is merely fair, due to 'Abd Allah ibn Salih al-Juhani.
[237]As in al-'Azim Abadi's commentary on this hadith in *'Awn al-Ma'bud* and others.
[238]Narrated from Abu Umama by al-Tabarani in *al-Kabir* (8:171) and al-Hakim (4:509-510, 1990 ed. 4:555) but al-Dhahabi said its sub-narrator 'Ufayr ibn Ma'dan is feeble *(wâhin)* – after al-Mundhiri in *al-Targhib* (1997 ed. 4:32) – and al-Haythami in *Majma' al-Zawa'id* (10:59) said he is weak. Shaykh Ahmad al-Ghumari in *al-Mughir* (p. 61) declares him a forger but al-Dhahabi reported no such position from the authorities in the *Mizan* (3:83 #5679), and Shaykh Ahmad in the same book (p. 104) declares his conviction that even the two *Sahihs* contain some forged narrations!

of my Community shall enter Paradise without reckoning nor punishment."[239]

40. Haram ibn Hayyan asked Uways al-Qarani: "Where do you advise me to go?" Uways replied: "To *Shâm*." Haram asked: "How is one's livelihood there?" Uways said: "Fie upon such hearts! Doubt has mixed into them and admonition is wasted on them."[240]

41. 'Ata' al-Khurasani said: "When I decided to move, I consulted those of the people of knowledge who were in Mecca, Madina, Kufa, Basra, and Khurasan, asking them where they thought I should go with my dependents. All of them said: 'You must go to *Shâm*.'"[241]

42. 'Abd Allah ibn Shawdhab said: "We spoke about *Shâm* and I said to Abu Sahl[242]: 'Have you not heard that such-and-such would take place in it?' He replied: 'Yes, but whatever takes place in it is lesser than what takes place elsewhere.'"[243]

---

[239]Narrated from Abu Umama by al-Tabarani in *al-Kabir* (8:194) with a chain containing 'Abd al-'Aziz ibn 'Ubayd Allah al-Himsi whom al-Haythami in *Majma' al-Zawa'id* (10:59) said is weak. The hadith is cited by al-Suyuti in *al-Jami' al-Saghir* and by al-Munawi in its commentary *Fayd al-Qadir* with the wording: Verily, three batches *(hathayât)* of my Community shall enter Paradise without reckoning nor punishment." Shaykh Ahmad al-Ghumari in *al-Mughir* declared it forged like the precedent narration, but al-Dhahabi in the *Mizan* (2:632) reported no such grading on 'Abd al-'Aziz ibn 'Ubayd Allah.
[240]Cited by al-Munawi in *Fayd al-Qadir* (4:170-171).
[241]Cited by Ibn 'Abd al-Salam in *Targhib Ahl al-Islam* (p. 17).
[242]This is Kathir ibn Ziyad al-Bursani al-Basri al-Balkhi.
[243]Cited by Ibn 'Abd al-Salam in *Targhib Ahl al-Islam* (p. 18).

IV.
The Vision of Allah ﷻ *

Ibn 'Abd al-Barr in *al-Intiqa'* and others relate that Malik and al-Shafi'i adduced as proof of the believers' vision of Allah ﷻ in the hereafter the verses: ❲That day will faces be resplendent, Looking toward their Lord❳ (75:22-23) and ❲Nay! Verily, from their Lord, that day, shall they [the transgressors] be veiled❳ (83:15).[244]

Imam Ibn Khafif stated in his *al-'Aqida al-Sahiha*:

30. The believers shall see Allah on the Day of Resurrection just as they see the full moon on the nights when it rises. They will not be unfairly deprived of seeing Him.

31. They will see Him without encompassment *(ihâta)* nor delimitation *(tahdîd)* within any given limit *(hadd)*, whether from the front, the back, above, below, right, or left. ...

97. Sight in the world is impossible.

The *Mu'tazila* and some other groups held that Allah could not be seen at all, even on the Day of Resurrection. They rejected the sound hadiths to the contrary, claiming that such

---

* This is the second version of a text previously published with our translation of Ibn Khafif's *al-'Aqida al-Sahiha* ("Correct Islamic Doctrine").

[244]Both Pickthall's and Yusuf 'Ali's translations parenthetically annul the meaning of Allah's vision, respectively: ❲Nay, but surely on that day they will be covered from (the mercy of) their Lord❳ and ❲Verily, from (the Light of) their Lord, that Day, will they be veiled❳.

vision necessitated corporeality and direction, which were precluded for Him. *Ahl al-Sunna* adduced the verse ❴**That day will
faces be resplendent, Looking toward their Lord**❵ (75:22-23)
and the mass-narrated hadiths to the effect that such vision will
be real. In contrast to the *Mu'tazila*, the totality of the scholars of
Ahl al-Sunna both excluded modalities of encompassment, delimitation, direction, and other corporeal qualities and, at the
same time, held that Allah will be seen by the believers in the
Hereafter without specifying how. However, they differed
whether such unqualified sight was possible in the world as well.

Al-Qari and al-Haytami reported that the agreement of *Ahl
al-Sunna* is that sight of Allah in the world is possible but that it
does not take place (except for the Prophet ﷺ), while two
contrary opinions on the topic are narrated from al-Ash'ari in al-
Qushayri's *Risala*.[245] The proof that His sight is possible in the
world was adduced from Musa's ﷺ request to Allah: ❴**My
Lord! Show me Your Self, that I may gaze upon You**❵
(7:143) as Prophets do not ask the impossible.[246] Imam al-
Qushayri stated in the *Risala* that sight of Allah in the world
does not take place for anyone except the Prophet ﷺ while al-
Dhahabi, conceding that sight of Allah in the world is possible,
held that it does not take place even for the Prophet ﷺ.[247] The
best statement on the issue is that of Shaykh Muhyi al-Din ibn
'Arabi: "He can be seen with the hearts and the eyes, if He so
wills."[248] Most or all of these views are based on the Prophet's

---

[245] Al-Qari, *al-Mirqat* (1892 ed. 5:303); al-Haytami, *Fatawa Hadithiyya*
(p. 147-150). The latter said (p. 150): "If it is authenticated that al-
Ash'ari held that the vision does take place in the world, then that
position is ignored as he either did not know of the Consensus to the
contrary, or took an anomalous *(shâdhdh)* stance which cannot be
taken into consideration."
[246] As stated by al-Qari in *Sharh al-Fiqh al-Akbar*.
[247] In the *Siyar* (8:430-431).
[248] In *al-Futuhat al-Makkiyya* (1:164 §142).

🕌 hadith: "Verily, you shall not see Allah until you die."[249] Ibn Hajar adduced the hadith: "Worship Allah as if you see Him" as further proof that there is no sight of Allah with the eyes of the head in this world but added: "The Prophet's 🕌 sight of Allah is supported by other evidence."[250]

The Prophet 🕌 saw Allah before death as is the doctrine of the majority of *Ahl al-Sunna* thus related from al-Nawawi by al-Qari.[251] The evidence for this is the hadith of Ibn 'Abbas whereby the Prophet 🕌 said: "I saw my Lord" *(ra'aytu rabbi)*.[252] Ibn Kathir cited it in his commentary on Sura al-Najm and declared its chain sound, but considered it part of the hadith of the dream cited below. Ibn al-Qayyim [see excerpt below] relates that Imam Ahmad considered such sight to be in the Prophet's 🕌 sleep but remains a true sight – as the dreams of

---

[249]Narrated from Abu Umama ibn al-Samit al-Bahili as part of a longer hadith by Ahmad with a sound chain, as stated by al-Zayn, in the *Musnad* (16:415 #22663), Ibn Majah, al-Nasa'i in *al-Sunan al-Kubra* (4:419 #7764), al-Hakim (4:456) who stated that it is *sahih* and al-Dhahabi concurred, Ibn Abi 'Asim in *al-Ahad wa al-Mathani* (2:446 #1249) and *al-Sunna* (p. 186-187 #429) with a sound chain as stated by al-Albani, al-Ajurri in *al-Shari'a*, and Ibn Khuzayma in *al-Tawhid*. It is also narrated without mention of the Companion's name by Muslim in his *Sahih*, al-Tirmidhi who declared it *hasan sahih*, Ahmad with a sound chain (17:72 #23562), and Ibn Abi 'Asim in *al-Sunna* (p. 187 #430) with a sound chain.
[250]In *Fath al-Bari* (1959 ed. 1:125 #50).
[251]In *al-Mirqat* (1892 ed. 5:308).
[252]Narrated by Ahmad with two chains of which one is sound, and al-Ajurri with a sound chain as stated by the editors of the former's *Musnad* (3:165 #2580, 3:184 #2634) and the latter's *al-Shari'a* (p. 495 #1047) as well as al-Haythami in *Majma' al-Zawa'id* (1:78-79). Also narrated by Ibn Abi 'Asim in *al-Sunna* (p. 188 #433) with the same chain as the second of Imam Ahmad's two narrations. Ahmad and Abu Zur'a considered this hadith authentic, as stated in *Tabaqat al-Hanabila* (1:312, 1:242), al-Suyuti's *al-La'ali'* (1:29-30), and al-Diya' al-Maqdisi's *al-Mukhtara* (1:79 #66).

Prophets are true – and that some of the Imam's companions
mistakenly attributed to him the position that the Prophet ﷺ saw
his Lord "with the eyes of his head."[253]

Al-Bayhaqi also narrated the hadith "I saw my Lord" in
al-Asma' wa al-Sifat with a sound chain but with the addition:
"in the form of a curly-haired, beardless young man wearing a
green robe," a condemned, disauthenticated addition and con-
catenation with another hadith that refers to Gibrîl ﷺ.[254] Hence
al-Suyuti interpreted it either as a dream or, quoting his shaykh
Ibn al-Humam, as "the veil of form" *(hijâb al-sûra).*[255]

The latter explanation is echoed in al-Qari's several
commentaries of the similar hadith whereby the Prophet ﷺ said:
"My Lord came to me in the best form – the narrator said: I
think he said: 'in my sleep' – and asked me over what did the
Higher Assembly *(al-mala' al-a'lâ)*[256] vie, and I said I did not
know, so He put His hand between my shoulders, and I felt its

---

[253]Ibn al-Qayyim, *Zad al-Ma'ad* (3:34). On the difference between the
dreams of Prophets and others, see al-'Iraqi, *Tarh al-Tathrib* (4:180-
184, 8:204-220).
[254]*Al-Asma' wa al-Sifat*, Kawthari ed. (p. 444-445), al-Hashidi ed.
(2:363-364 #938). A "condemned" *(munkar)* narration according to
Imam Ahmad as stated in al-Dhahabi's *Tartib al-Mawdu'at* (p. 22
#22), and according to al-Ahdab in *Zawa'id Tarikh Baghdad* (8:37-40
#1662). Ibn al-Jawzi in *Daf' Shubah al-Tashbih* (1998 Kawthari repr.
p. 34) states that the hadith is narrated through Hammad ibn Salama
and that his foster-son the *zindîq* Ibn Abi al-'Awja' used to interpolate
this kind of baseless narrations into his books. Al-Dhahabi also states
that it is *munkar* in the *Siyar* (8:430-431), however, he seems to apply
this condemnation to the entirety of the narrations in this chapter.
[255]In *al-La'ali'* (1:29-30).
[256]I.e. "the angels brought near" according to Ibn al-Athir in *al-Nihaya*
and others.

coolness in my innermost, and knowledge of all things between the East and the West came to me."[257]

---

[257]Narrated by al-Tirmidhi with three chains, all *sahîh* according to al-Albani: two from Ibn 'Abbas – in the first of which he said "the knowledge of all things in the heaven and the earth" while he graded the second *hasan gharîb* – and one chain from Mu'adh *(hasan sahîh)* which explicitly mentions that this took place in the Prophet's ﷺ sleep. Al-Bukhari declared the latter chain *sahîh* as stated by al-Tirmidhi in his *Sunan* and in his *'Ilal*, and it towers over all other chains, according to Ibn Hajar in *al-Isaba* (2:397), in the facts that there is no discrepancy over it among the hadith scholars and its text is undisputed (cf. al-Bayhaqi, *al-Asma' wa al-Sifat*, al-Hashidi ed. 2:78). Also narrated by Ahmad with four sound chains according to Shakir and al-Zayn: one from Ibn 'Abbas with the words "I think he said: 'in my sleep'" (3:458 #3484); one from Mu'adh which Ahmad explicitly declared *sahîh* as narrated by Ibn 'Adi in *al-Kamil* (6:2244), with the words: "I woke up and lo! I was with my Lord" (16:200 #22008); and two from unnamed Companions in which no mention is made of the Prophet's ﷺ sleep or wakefulness (13:93-94 #16574, 16:556 #23103). Al-Haythami declared the latter sound as well as other chains cited by al-Tabarani in *al-Kabir* (20:109 #216, 20:141 #290) and al-Bazzar in his *Musnad*, and he declared fair the chain narrated from Abu Umama by al-Tabarani in *al-Kabir* (8:290 #8117). See *Majma' al-Zawa'id* (7:176-179). Shaykhs 'Abd al-Qadir and Shu'ayb al-Arna'ut both declared *sahîh* the seven narrations of al-Tirmidhi and Ahmad in their edition of Ibn al-Qayyim's *Zad al-Ma'ad* (3:33-34 n. 4). Also narrated from Jabir ibn Samura by Ibn Abi 'Asim in *al-Sunna* (p. 203 #465) with a fair chain according to al-Albani. Also narrated from 'Abd al-Rahman ibn 'A'ish by al-Darimi in his *Musnad* (2:170 #2149) and al-Tabarani through two chains in *al-Ahad wa al-Mathani* (5:48-50 #2585-2586) and another in *Musnad al-Shamiyyin* (1:339 #597), and from Umm al-Tufayl by al-Tabarani in *al-Ahad* (6:158 #3385). The latter chain actually states: "I saw my Lord in the best form of a beardless young man" and was rejected by al-Dhahabi in *Tahdhib al-Mawdu'at* (p. 22 #22). Also narrated from the Companion Abu Rafi' [*al-Isaba* 7:134 #9875] by al-Tabarani in *al-Kabir* (1:317 #938). Also narrated from Ibn 'Abbas by Abu Ya'la in his *Musnad* (4:475 #2608). Some fair narrations of this hadith – such as al-Tabarani's from 'Abd al-Rahman ibn 'Iyash and al-Khatib's from Abu 'Ubayda ibn al-Jarrah in *Tarikh Baghdad* (8:151) – have the words: "I saw my Lord" instead

Al-Mubarakfuri relates from Ibn Kathir and al-Haytami the position that the above vision took place in the Prophet's ﷺ sleep. This is also the position of Ibn al-Jawzi based on what he termed the best chains of this hadith.[258] Al-Haytami points out that the words "I woke up and saw my Lord" in Ahmad's narration from Mu'adh are actually changed from "I dozed off and saw my Lord" due to a copyist's corruption of "I dozed off" *(istathqaltu)* – as in al-Tirmidhi's narration from Mu'adh – into "I woke up" *(istayqaztu).*[259] On the whole, the scholars' interpretations of the Prophet's ﷺ vision show that whether it took place in his dream or in a wakeful state, "with the eyes of the heart" or "with the eyes of the head," does not change the fact that he saw Him in the real sense, as the Prophet's ﷺ dream-vision or heart-vision is by far sharper, more accurate, and more real than the visions of ordinary people.

---

of "My Lord came to me," hence Ibn Kathir's conclusion previously cited. Al-Ahdab in *Zawa'id Tarikh Baghdad* (6:251-253) and al-Haytami also cited Abu 'Ubayda ibn al-Jarrah, Ibn 'Umar, Abu Hurayra, Anas, Thawban, and Abu Umama which brings to at least eleven (without Umm al-Tufayl) the number of Companions who narrated this hadith. The various chains and narrations of this hadith were collated and discussed by Ibn Rajab in his monograph *Ikhtiyar al-Awla fi Sharh Hadith Ikhtisam al-Mala' al-A'la*, ed. Jasim al-Dawsari (Kuwait: Dar al-Aqsa, 1406). See also: Ibn Athir, *Jami' al-Usul* (9:548-550). Among those that considered this hadith as falling below the grade of *sahih* are al-Bayhaqi in *al-Asma' wa al-Sifat* (Kawthari ed. p. 300, al-Hashidi ed. 2:72-79), Ibn al-Jawzi in *al-'Ilal al-Mutanahiya* (1:34), Ibn Khuzayma in *al-Tawhid* (p. 214-221) and al-Daraqutni in his *'Ilal* (6:56). Some went too far and suggested that it was forged: see al-Saqqaf, *Aqwal al-Huffaz al-Manthura li Bayan Wad' Hadith Ra'aytu Rabbi fi Ahsani Sura*, appended to his edition of Ibn al-Jawzi's *Daf' Shubah al-Tashbih.*
[258]In *Daf' Shubah al-Tashbih* (Kawthari ed. p. 32).
[259]In Al-Mubarakfuri *Tuhfa al-Ahwadhi* (9:74).

Ahl al-Sunna scholars gave many interpretations of the above hadith. For example, al-Razi and, before him, al-Bayhaqi, interpreted the placing of Allah's Hand as His extreme consideration and attention to the Prophet ﷺ, or as His immense favor to him, while its specific placing between his shoulders refers to the pouring of divine kindness and mercy into his heart, and the coolness refers to the completion and perfection of his knowledge as shown by his words "I knew all things between the East and the West."[260] Al-Qari wrote the following in the chapter on the Prophet's ﷺ turban in his book *Jam' al-Wasa'il fi Sharh al-Shama'il*, a commentary on al-Tirmidhi's *Shama'il* or "Characteristics of the Prophet":

> Whether the Prophet ﷺ saw his Lord in his sleep or whether Allah the Glorious and Exalted manifested Himself to him with a form *(bi al-tajallî al-sûrî)*, this type of manifestation is known among the masters of spiritual states and stations *(arbâb al-hâl wa al-maqâm)*, and it consists in being reminded of His disposition *(hay'atihi)* and reflecting upon His vision *(ru'yatihi)*, which is the outcome of the perfection of one's self-detachment *(takhliyatihi)* and self-adornment *(tahliyatihi)*. And Allah knows best about the states of His Prophets and Intimate Friends whom He has raised with His most excellent upbringing, and the mirrors of whose hearts He has polished with His most excellent polish, until they witnessed the Station of Divine Presence and Abiding *(maqâm al-hudûr wa al-baqâ')*, and they rid themselves of the rust of screens and extinction *(sada' al-huzûr wa al-fanâ')*. May Allah bestow on us their yearnings, may He make us taste their states and manners, and may He make

---

[260] Al-Razi, *Asas al-Taqdis*, as quoted by al-Kawthari in *Daf' Shubah al-Tashbih* (p. 32-33 n.). Cf. al-Bayhaqi, *al-Asma' wa al-Sifat* (p. 300-301).

us die in the condition of loving them and raise us in their group.[261]

Al-Qari goes on to quote Ibn al-Qayyim's relation from Ibn Taymiyya that when the Prophet ﷺ saw that his Lord put His hand between his shoulders, he honored that place with the extremity of the turban. Elsewhere he states:

> Ibn Sadaqa said that Abu Zur'a said: 'The hadith of Ibn 'Abbas [about the Prophet seeing His Lord] is sound *(sahîh)*, and none denies it except a *Mu'tazili'...* Ibn al-Humam said: 'This is but the veil of form *(hijâb al-sûra)*.' It seems that he meant by this that the entire goal can be visualized if it is interpreted as a figural manifestation *(tajallî sûrî)*, as it is of necessity absurd to interpret it as a real or literal manifestation *(tajallî haqiqî)*. Allah Almighty has many forms of manifestations *(anwâ' min al-tajalliyât)* according to His Entity and Attributes. Likewise, He possesses all power and encompassing ability, well beyond the angels and other than them, to fashion forms and appearances. Yet He is transcendent above possessing a body *(jism)*, a form *(sûra)*, and directions *(jihât)* with regard to His Entity. These considerations help solve many of the purported difficulties in the ambiguous verses and the narrations of the Attributes. Allah knows best the reality of spiritual stations and the minutiae of objectives.... If the hadith is shown to have something in its chain that indicates forgery, then fine; otherwise: the door of figurative interpretation is wide and imposes itself *(bâb al-ta'wîl wâsi'un muhattam)*.[262]

---

[261] Al-Qari, *Jam' al-Wasa'il* (p. 209).
[262] Al-Qari, *al-Asrar al-Marfu'a* (2nd ed. p. 209-210 #209; 1st ed. p. 126 #478).

Elsewhere al-Qari states:

> If this vision took place in dream, then there is no
> difficulty.... However, if it took place in a wakeful state
> *(fi al-yaqaza)*, as conveyed by the letter of Ahmad ibn
> Hanbal's narration [but see al-Haytami's comment quoted
> above], then the *Salaf* declared belief in the letter of such
> narrations – provided they were sound – without
> explaining them as one would explain the attributes of
> creatures. Rather, they negated modality *(al-kayfiyya)* and
> entrusted knowledge of their hidden meaning to Allah. For
> He shows to His Prophet ﷺ whatever He wishes from
> behind the curtains of the Unseen, including what our
> minds have no way of comprehending. However, to leave
> aside figurative interpretation *(al-ta'wîl)* in our time
> fosters confusion *(fitna)* in the beliefs of people, due to the
> dissemination of the doctrines of misguidance *(i'tiqâdât
> al-dalâl)*. Therefore, it is appropriate to interpret it in
> conformity with the Law as a possible intrepretation, not a
> definitive one. Accordingly, the words 'in the best form'
> could signify 'I saw my Lord as I was in the best form in
> the sense of His utmost favor and kindness to me'; or 'in
> the Lord's best form' in the sense that the form of
> something is whatever distinguishes it from something
> else, whether it pertains to the thing itself or to whatever
> part of it is being characterized. This can be applied to
> meanings just as it is applied to material bodies. One
> speaks about 'picturing a matter or a situation thus.'
> Allah's 'form' – and Allah knows best – would then be
> His specific Entity *(dhâtuhu al-makhsûsa)* separate from
> any other representation of the farthest levels of perfec-
> tion, or the Attribute that is specific to Him, meaning 'My

143

Lord was more gracious and kinder than at any other time.' Thus did al-Tibi and al-Tawrabashti relate it.[263]

The above is reminiscent of Ibn al-Jawzi's similar interpretation in the second hadith of his *Daf' Shubah al-Tashbih*:

> If we say that he 🕌 saw Him while awake, then the form, if we say that it refers to Allah Almighty, would mean: "I saw Him in the best of His Attributes in turning to me and being pleased with me." If we say that it refers to the Prophet 🕌 himself, then it would mean: "I saw Him as I was in the best form."[264]

Others considered Ibn 'Abbas' narration to refer to a vision with the eyes of the heart, as elucidated by Ibn 'Abbas' other narrations in *Sahih Muslim* and al-Tirmidhi *(hasan)*: "He saw him with his heart." Another narration from Ibn 'Abbas in Muslim states: "He saw him with his heart twice," in commentary of the verses: ❨**The heart lied not (in seeing) what it saw**❩ (53:11), ❨**And verily he saw him, yet another time**❩ (53:13).

---

[263] Al-Qari, *al-Mirqat* (1892 ed. 5:303). Al-Mubarakfuri in *Tuhfa al-Ahwadhi* (9:73-74) rejects al-Qari's words "to leave aside figurative interpretation in our time fosters confusion due to the dissemination of the doctrines of misguidance" on the grounds that they contravene – in his view – the method of the *Salaf*, a proof of al-Mubarakfuri's leaning towards unenlightened literalism. Al-Shatibi said in *al-Muwafaqat* (2:332): "The Congregation of [Sunni] Muslims follow Imam Malik's position [in the detestation of *kalâm*], except if one is obliged to speak. One must not remain silent if his purpose is to refute falsehood and guide people away from it, or if one fears the spread of misguidance or some similar danger."
[264] Ibn al-Jawzi, *Daf' Shubah al-Tashbih* (Kawthari ed. p. 32).

Another explanation is that the Prophet ﷺ saw light. This is stated explicitly in the Prophet's ﷺ reply, when asked by Abu Dharr if he had actually seen his Lord: "I saw light."[265]

Many sound reports show that the Companions differed sharply whether the Prophet ﷺ saw Allah or not. Ibn 'Abbas related that he did, while Ibn Mas'ud, 'A'isha, Abu Hurayra, and Abu Dharr related reports to the contrary, stating that the verses of Sura al-Najm and other Suras referred to Gibrîl ﷺ,[266] and that the Prophet ﷺ said that he saw light.

Al-Bukhari narrated from Masruq that the latter said:

I said to 'A'isha: "O my mother! Did Muhammad ﷺ see his Lord?" She replied: "My hair stands on end because of what you said. Have you no idea of three things – whoever tells them to you is lying? [First,] whoever tells you that Muhammad ﷺ saw his Lord, is lying." She then recited: **❰Vision comprehends Him not, but He comprehends (all) vision. He is the Subtle, the Aware.❱** (6:103) **❰And it was not (vouchsafed) to any mortal that Allah should speak to him unless (it be) by revelation or from behind a veil❱** (42:51). "[Second,] whoever tells you that he knows what shall happen tomorrow, is lying." She then recited: **❰No soul knows what it will earn tomorrow❱** (31:34). "And [third,] whoever tells you that he concealed something, is lying." She then recited: **❰O Messenger! Make known that which has been revealed unto you from your Lord, for if you do it not, you will not have conveyed His message. Allah will protect you from mankind. Lo! Allah guides not the**

---

[265]Narrated by Muslim, al-Tirmidhi *(hasan)*, and Ahmad through four chains.
[266]As stated by Ibn al-Qayyim in *Zad al-Ma'ad* (3:34).

145

disbelieving folk.⟩ (5:67) "However, he did see Gibrîl ﷺ in his actual form twice."

This hadith is also narrated from Masruq by Muslim thus:

I was sitting back in 'A'isha's house when she said: "O Abu 'A'isha [i.e. Masruq], there are three things, whoever says any of which, he is lying about Allah in the most hateful manner." I asked: "Which things?" She said: "[First,] whoever tells you that Muhammad ﷺ saw his Lord, he is lying about Allah in the most hateful manner." I was sitting back, so I sat up and said: "O Mother of the Believers! Give me a moment and do not rush me. Did not Allah Almighty say: **⟨Surely he beheld him on the clear horizon⟩** (81:23), **⟨And verily he saw him, yet another time⟩** (53:13)?" She replied: "I am the first in this entire Community to have asked Allah's Messenger ﷺ about this, and he said: 'It is but Gibrîl, I did not see him in the actual form in which he was created other than these two times. I saw him alighting from the heaven, covering it all. The magnitude of his frame spans what lies between the heaven and the earth.'" Then she said: "Did you not hear Allah say: **⟨Vision comprehends Him not, but He comprehends (all) vision. He is the Subtle, the Aware⟩** (6:103)? Did you not hear Allah say: **⟨And it was not (vouchsafed) to any mortal that Allah should speak to him unless (it be) by revelation or from behind a veil, or (that) He sends a messenger to reveal what He will by His leave. Lo! He is Exalted, Wise⟩** (42:51)?" She continued: "[Second,] whoever claims that Allah's Messenger ﷺ concealed any part of Allah's Book, he is lying about Allah in the most hateful manner when Allah is saying: **⟨O Messenger! Make known that which has been revealed unto you from your Lord, for if you do it not, you will not have conveyed His message⟩** (5:67)."

146

She continued: "[Third,] whoever claims that he can tell what shall happen tomorrow, he is lying about Allah in the most hateful manner, since Allah is saying: ❨Say: None in the heavens and the earth knows the Unseen save Allah [and they know not when they will be raised again]❩ (27:65)."[267]

Muslim mentions another wording which adds the phrase:

She said: "If Muhammad 𝕴 had concealed anything of what was revealed to him, he would have concealed this verse: ❨And when you said unto him on whom Allah has conferred favor and you have conferred favor: Keep your wife to yourself, and fear Allah. And you did hide in your mind that which Allah was to bring to light, and you did fear mankind whereas Allah had a better right that you should fear Him❩ (33:37)."

A narration by al-Tirmidhi from al-Sha'bi cites the two positions in context:

Ibn 'Abbas met Ka'b [al-Ahbar] in 'Arafa and asked him about something, whereupon Ka'b began to shout *Allahu Akbar!* until the mountains answered him. Ibn 'Abbas said: "We are the Banu Hashim!"[268] Ka'b said: "Allah 𝕴 has apportioned His vision and His speech between Muhammad 𝕴 and Musa ﷺ. Musa ﷺ spoke

---

[267] Also narrated from Masruq by al-Tirmidhi *(hasan sahîh)*.

[268] Al-Tibi said: "[Ibn 'Abbas said] this in order to urge him to be quiet, stop his irritation, and reflect upon the answer, meaning: 'We are people of science and knowledge, we do not ask about things which should be considered so far-fetched.' Because of this, he reflected and gave him his answer." In al-Mubarakfuri, *Tuhfa al-Ahwadhi* (9:118 #3496).

with Him twice and Muhammad ﷺ saw him twice."
Masruq said: "Later[269] I went to visit 'A'isha and asked:
'Did Muhammad see his Lord?' She replied: 'You have
said something that makes my hair stand on end.' I said:
'Do not rush!' and recited [the verses which conclude
with][270] the verse {Verily he saw one of the greater
revelations of his Lord} (53:18). She said: 'Where is this
taking you? It was but Gibrîl. Whoever tells you that
Muhammad ﷺ saw his Lord, or concealed something
which he was commanded [to reveal], or knew the five
things which Allah mentioned {Lo! Allah! With Him is
knowledge of the Hour. He sends down the rain [and
knows that which is in the wombs. No soul knows what
it will earn tomorrow, and no soul knows in what land
it will die. Lo! Allah is Knower, Aware]} (31:34) – he
has told an enormous lie. Rather, he saw Gibrîl, whom he
did not see in his actual form except twice: once at the
Lote-Tree of the Farthest Boundary *(sidra al-muntaha)*,
and once in Jiyâd [in Mecca], with his six hundred wings,
he had filled the firmament."

Ibn al-Qayyim in *Zad al-Ma'ad* said:

The Companions differed whether the Prophet ﷺ
actually saw his Lord that night [of *isrâ'* and *mi'râj*] or
not. It is authentically narrated from Ibn 'Abbas that the

---

[269]Al-Tibi said: "It appears from this wording that Masruq was present
at the time of the exchange that took place between Ka'b and Ibn
'Abbas." In al-Mubarakfuri, *Tuhfa al-Ahwadhi* (9: 119).
[270]This gloss is by al-Tibi, who said: "It is confirmed by al-Tirmidhi's
other narration stating: 'O Mother of the Believers! Give me a moment
and do not rush me. Did not Allah Almighty say: {And verily he saw
him, yet another time} (53:13), {Surely he beheld him on the clear
horizon} (81:23)?'" Al-Mubarakfuri confirmed al-Tibi's reading. In
Tuhfa al-Ahwadhi (9: 119).

Prophet ﷺ saw his Lord, and also authentically related
that Ibn 'Abbas said: "He saw Him with his heart." It is
also authentically related from 'A'isha and Ibn Mas'ud
that they denied such vision, saying that Allah's words
❰And verily he saw him, yet another time, at the Lote
Tree of the Farthest Boundary❱ (53:13) refer to Gibrîl
الْعَلَيْه.[271] It is also authentically related from Abu Dharr that
the latter asked the Prophet ﷺ: "Did you see your Lord?"
and he replied: "[I saw] a huge light, how could I see
Him?" *(nûrun annâ arâh?)*. That is: light came in between
myself and His sight, as stated in the wording: "I saw
light" *(ra'aytu nûran)*.[272] 'Uthman ibn Sa'id al-Darimi
said that the Companions all agreed that the Prophet ﷺ
did not see Him.[273] Shaykh al-Islam Ibn Taymiyya – may
Allah sanctify his soul! – said:

> Ibn 'Abbas's statement that "He saw Him"
> does not contradict that claim, nor his statement that
> "He saw Him with his heart." For it is also
> authentically related that the Prophet ﷺ said: "I saw
> my Lord – glorified and exalted is He!"[274] However,
> the latter was not during the *isrâ'* but in Madina,
> when the Prophet ﷺ was occupied and could not be
> with the Companions at the time of the dawn
> prayer, after which he told them about his vision of
> Allah during his sleep that night. It is on that
> evidence that Imam Ahmad based himself when he
> said: "Yes, he saw him in reality *(na'am ra'âhu*

---

[271]'A'isha's stance is narrated by al-Bukhari in four places, Muslim,
and al-Tirmidhi; Ibn Mas'ud's, by Bukhari and Muslim.
[272]Narrated by Muslim.
[273]This is flatly contradicted by the reports of Ibn 'Abbas, but Ibn al-
Qayyim does not reject it out of deference for Ibn Taymiyya, who
defends al-Darimi's claim.
[274]See above, n. 252.

haqqan), for the dream-visions of Prophets are real." This is absolutely true, but Ahmad did not say that he saw Him with the eyes of his head while awake. Whoever said that he did, is mistaken. Ahmad said one time: "He saw Him" and another time: "He saw Him with his heart." These are the two statements narrated from him on the issue. The third statement whereby "He saw Him with the eyes of his head" comes from the free paraphrase of some of his companions. Ahmad's texts are present with us, and nowhere are such words found in them.[275]

Ibn Hajar analyzed this issue at length in his works[276] and compiled a monograph on the topic titled *al-Ghunya fi al-Ru'ya.*[277] Al-Qari also gave an authoritative discussion of the topic in *al-Mirqat.*[278]

---

[275]In Ibn al-Qayyim, *Zad al-Ma'ad* (3:33-34).
[276]Cf. *Fath al-Bari* (1959 ed. 1:125-135 #50, 8:608-610, 11:463-469 #6204) and *al-Isaba* (2:405-406).
[277]This work is briefly described in 'Abd al-Mun'im's *Ibn Hajar* (1:267-268).
[278]*Al-Mirqat* (1892 ed. 5:306f.).

Appendix

The Hadith
"Whoever Visits My Grave,
My Intercession Is Guaranteed For Him"

The hadith "Whoever visits my grave, my intercession will be guaranteed for him" *(Man zâra qabrî wajabat lahu shafâ'atî)*[279] is a fair *(hasan)* narration as concluded by Imam

---

[279]Narrated from Ibn 'Umar by al-Daraqutni in his *Sunan* (2:278 #194), Abu Dawud al-Tayalisi in his *Musnad* (2:12), al-Dulabi in *al-Kuna wa al-Asma'* (2:64), al-Khatib in *Talkhis al-Mutashabih fi al-Rasm* (1:581), Ibn al-Dubaythi in *al-Dhayl 'ala al-Tarikh* (2:170), Ibn Abi al-Dunya in *Kitab al-Qubur*, al-Bayhaqi in *Shu'ab al-Iman* (3:490), al-Hakim al-Tirmidhi in *Nawadir al-Usul* (p. 148), al-Haythami in *Majma' al-Zawa'id* (4:2), al-Subki in *Shifa' al-Siqam* (p. 12-14), Abu al-Shaykh, Ibn 'Adi in *al-Kamil* (6:235, 6:351), al-'Uqayli in *al-Du'afa'* (4:170), al-Bazzar in his *Musnad* with a very weak chain containing 'Abd Allah ibn Ibrahim al-Ghifari [cf. Ibn Hajar's *Mukhtasar* (1:481 #822)] with the wording "my intercession shall take place for him" *(hallat lahu shafâ'atî)*, and Ibn Hajar who indicated its grade of *hasan* in *Talkhis al-Habir* (2:266) as it is strengthened by other hadiths which both he and al-Haythami mention, such as:
- "Whoever visits me without any avowed purpose other than my visit, it is incumbent upon me to be his intercessor on the Day of Resurrection." Narrated by al-Tabarani in *al-Awsat* and *al-Kabir* with a chain containing Muslima ibn Salim and by Ibn al-Sakan in his *Sunan al-Sihah* as stated by al-Shirbini in *Mughni al-Muhtaj* (1:512).
- "Whoever makes pilgrimage then visits me after my death it is as if he visited me in my life." Narrated by al-Tabarani in *al-Kabir* (12:406) and al-Daraqutni (2:278) with a chain containing Hafs ibn Abi Dawud al-Qari, whom only Ahmad declared passable *(sâlih)*.
- "Whoever visits my grave after my death is as those who visited me in my life." Narrated by al-Tabarani in *al-Kabir* (12:406) and *al-Awsat* (1:94) with a chain containing 'A'isha bint Yunus, whose

Abu al-Hasanat al-Lacknawi[280] and his student 'Abd al-Fattah Abu Ghudda in the latter's notes on Imam Malik's *Muwatta'* according to Muhammad ibn al-Hasan's narration (chapter 49: On the Grave of the Prophet 鸞) as well as Shaykh Mahmud Mamduh,[281] although some early scholars had declared it sound *(sahih)* such as Ibn al-Sakan in *al-Sunan al-Sihah* and 'Abd al-Haqq al-Ishbili in *al-Ahkam,* followed by *Shaykh al-Islam* al-Taqi al-Subki in *Shifa' al-Siqam* in view of the totality of the chains.[282] Other hadith scholars who considered it authentic are Ibn Hajar's student the hadith master al-Sakhawi,[283] the hadith master of Madina al-Samhudi,[284] and Shaykh al-Islam al-Haytami in *al-Jawhar al-Munazzam.* Al-Ghassani (d. 682) did not include it in his compendium of al-Daraqutni's weak narrations entitled *Takhrij al-Ahadith al-Di'af min Sunan al-Daraqutni.*[285] Some late scholars, beginning with Ibn Taymiyya, remained undecided whether to grade this hadith weak or forged.

---

status is uncertain, and from Hatib by al-Daraqutni (2:278) with another chain which al-Dhahabi said was one of the best chains in that chapter. Abu Ghudda cites a fourth narration:

- "Whoever makes pilgrimage and does not visit me, has been rude to me." Narrated by al-Daraqutni in his *Sunan.* Abu Ghudda said: "It is not forged as Ibn al-Jawzi and Ibn Taymiyya said, rather, a number of scholars considered its chain fair, and a number considered it weak."

Al-'Uqayli in *al-Du'afa'* (4:170) declared the chains of Ibn 'Umar's narration "soft" *(layyina)* as did al-Dhahabi, the latter adding – as did al-Bayhaqi and al-Fattani in *Tadhkira al-Mawdu'at* – that they strengthened each other as none contains any liar nor forger, as stated by al-Suyuti in *al-Durar al-Muntathira,* al-Munawi in *Fayd al-Qadir,* and al-'Ajluni in *Kashf al-Khafa* (2:328-329).

[280]In *Zafar al-Amani* (p. 422) and *al-Ajwiba al-Fadila* (p. 155).
[281]In his *Raf' al-Minara* (p. 280 and p. 318).
[282]As related by Ibn Hajar in *Talkhis al-Habir* (2:267). Cf. al-Shawkani in *Nayl al-Awtar* (5:95) and al-Sindi in his notes on Ibn Majah.
[283]In *al-Qawl al-Badi'* (p. 160).
[284]In *Sa'ada al-Darayn* (1:77).
[285]Published at Ryad: Dar 'Alam al-Kutub, 1991.

Al-Lacknawi said about this hadith:

There are some who declared it weak [e.g. al-Bayhaqi, Ibn Khuzayma, and al-Suyuti], and others who asserted that all the hadiths on visitation of the Prophet 鬱 are forged, such as Ibn Taymiyya and his followers, but both positions are false for those who were given right understanding, for verification of the case dictates that the hadith is *hasan*, as Taqi al-Din al-Subki has expounded in his book *Shifa' al-Siqam fi Ziyara Khayr al-Anam.*"[286]

Among those who fall into the category of "Ibn Taymiyya and his followers" on this issue:

- Ibn 'Abd al-Hadi who wrote *al-Sarim al-Munki fi al-Radd 'ala al-Subki* in violent refutation of al-Subki's book on visitation but contradicted his own position in another book of his.[287] Shaykh Mahmud Mamduh refuted his weakening of this hadith in great detail[288] and stated that *al-Sarim al-Munki* is at the root of all subsequent generalizations in weakening the hadiths that concern the desirability of visitation.[289]

- the late Wahhabi shaykh 'Abd al-'Aziz Bin Baz who reiterated Ibn Taymiyya's imprudent verdict: "The hadiths that

---

[286]Al-Lacknawi, *Zafar al-Amani* (p. 422).

[287]Ibn 'Abd al-Hadi makes much ado about the reliability of 'Abd Allah ibn 'Umar al-'Umari in *al-Sarim al-Munki*, but relies upon him in another book, *al-Tanqih* (1:122) as pointed out by Mamduh in *Raf' al-Minara* (p. 12). Al-Samannudi refuted ibn 'Abd al-Hadi in his *Nusrat al-Imam al-Subki*.

[288]In *Raf' al-Minara* (p. 280-318).

[289]In *Raf' al-Minara* (p. 9).

concern the visitation of the grave of the Prophet ﷺ are all weak, indeed forged";[290]

- Nasir al-Albani,[291] who claimed that the visit to the Prophet ﷺ ranks among the innovations;[292]

- and Nasir al-Jadya', who in 1993 obtained his Ph.D. with First Honors from the University of Muhammad ibn Sa'ud after writing a 600-page book entitled *al-Tabarruk* in which he perpetuates the same aberrant claim.[293]

Al-Sakhawi said:

> The emphasis and encouragement on visiting his noble grave is mentioned in numerous hadiths, and it would suffice to show this if there was only the hadith whereby the truthful and God-confirmed Prophet promises that his intercession among other things becomes guaranteed for whoever visits him, and the Imams are in complete agreement from the time directly after his passing until our own time that this [i.e. visiting him] is among the best acts of drawing near to Allah.[294]

---

[290]In his annotations on Ibn Hajar's *Fath al-Bari* (1989 ed. 3:387), echoing the exact words used by Ibn Taymiyya in his *Minhaj al-Sunna al-Nabawiyya* (1986 ed. 2:441) and *Majmu'a al-Fatawa* (27:119).
[291]In his *Irwa' al-Ghalil* (4:337-338) in which he imitated Ibn 'Abd al-Hadi's claims.
[292]In *Talkhis Ahkam al-Jana'iz* (p. 110) and elsewhere in his writings.
[293]Nasir al-Jadya', *al-Tabarruk* (p. 322). Note that all these books are presently available in print, but not *Shifa' al-Siqam*!
[294]Al-Sakhawi, *al-Qawl al-Badi'* (p. 160). He contradicts himself in *al-Maqasid al-Hasana* (p. 413) where he adopts al-Dhahabi's opinion that "the chains of the hadith of visitation are all 'soft' *(layyina)* but strengthen each other because none of them contains any liar."

There is no contest among the jurists of the Four Schools as to the probative force of the narration of Ibn 'Umar, as it is adduced time and again by the jurists to support the strong desirability of visiting the Prophet 🕌 in Madina. See, for example, among Hanbali sources alone:

- Ibn Qudama's *al-Mughni* (3:297)
- Ibn Muflih's al-Mubdi' fi Sharh al-Muqni' (3:259)
- Al-Buhuti's *Kashshaf al-Qanna'* (2:515; 5:36)
- Ibn Dawyan's *Manar al-Sabil* (1:256).

See also the additional sources illustrating the visit to the Prophet 🕌, among them that of Bilal ibn Rabah al-Habashi all the way from *Shâm*, as well as the Companions' practice of seeking the Prophet 🕌 as a means for their needs by visiting his grave, such as Bilal ibn al-Harith al-Muzani, Abu Ayyub al-Ansari, and 'A'isha, all as cited in the sections on *Tawassul* and Visitation in Shaykh Hisham Kabbani's *Encyclopedia of Islamic Doctrine*. And Allah knows best.

Bibliography

'Abd al-Razzaq. *Al-Musannaf.* 11 vols. Ed. Habib al-Rahman al-A'zami. Beirut: al-Maktab al-Islami, 1983. With al-Azdi's *Kitab al-Jami'* as the last two volumes.

————. *Tafsir al-Qur'an.* 3 vols. Ed. Mustafa Muslim Muhammad. Riyadh: Maktaba al-Rushd, 1990.

Abu Dawud. *Sunan.* 3 vols. Ed. Muhammad Fouad 'Abd al-Baqi. Beirut: Dar al-Kutub al-'Ilmiyya, 1996. See also Al-'Azim Abadi, *'Awn al-Ma'bud.*

Abu Dawud al-Tayalisi, see al-Tayalisi.

Abu al-Su'ud. *Irshad al-'Aql al-Salim ila Mazaya al-Qur'an al-Karim.* 9 vols. Beirut: Dar Ihya' al-Turath al-'Arabi, n.d. Reprint.

Abu Ya'la al-Musili. *Musnad.* 13 vols. Ed. Husayn Salim Asad. Damascus: Dar al-Ma'mun li al-Turath, 1984.

Abu Nu'aym al-Asfahani. *Hilya al-Awliya' wa Tabaqat al-Asfiya'.* 12 vols. Ed. Mustafa 'Abd al-Qadir 'Ata. Beirut: Dar al-Kutub al-'Ilmiyya, 1997.

Al-Ahdab, Khaldun. *Zawa'id Tarikh Baghdad 'Ala al-Kutub al-Sitta.* 10 vols. Damascus: Dar al-Qalam, 1996.

Ahmad ibn Hanbal. *Fada'il al-Sahaba.* 2 vols. Ed. Wasi Allah Muhammad 'Abbas. Beirut: Mu'assasa al-Risala, 1983.

————. *Al-Musnad.* 20 vols. Ed. Ahmad Shakir and Hamza Ahmad al-Zayn. Cairo: Dar al-Hadith, 1995.

Al-'Ajluni. *Kashf al-Khafa.* 2nd ed. 2 vols. Beirut: Dar Ihya' al-Turath al-'Arabi, 1932.

Al-'Azim Abadi, Muhammad Shams al-Haqq. *'Awn al-Ma'bud Sharh Sunan Abi Dawud.* 14 vols. in 7. Beirut: Dar al-Kutub al-'Ilmiyya, n.d. Includes Abu Dawud's *Sunan.*

Al-Bayhaqi. *Dala'il al-Nubuwwa wa Ma'rifa Ahwal Sahib al-Shari'a.* 7 vols. Ed. 'Abd al-Mu'ti Amin Qal'aji. Beirut: Dar al-Kutub al-'Ilmiyya, 1985.

————. *Al-I'tiqad 'ala Madhhab al-Salaf Ahl al-Sunna wa al-Jama'a.* Beirut: Dar al-Afaq al-Jadida, 1981; Dar al-Kutub al-'Ilmiyya, 1986^2.

————. *Shu'ab al-Iman*. 8 vols. Ed. Muhammad Zaghlul. Beirut: Dar al-Kutub al-'Ilmiyya, 1990.

————. *Al-Sunan al-Kubra*. 10 vols. Ed. Muhammad 'Abd al-Qadir 'Ata. Mecca: Maktaba Dar al-Baz, 1994.

Al-Bukhari. *Al-Adab al-Mufrad*. 3rd ed. Ed. Muhammad Fu'ad 'Abd al-Baqi. Beirut: Dar al-Basha'ir al-Islamiyya, 1989.

————. *Sahih*. Ed. Ahmad 'Ali al-Siharanfuri. 1272/1856.

————. *Sahih*. 8 vols. in 3. Ed. Muhammad al-Zuhri al-Ghamrawi. Bulaq: al-Matba'a al-Kubra al-Amiriyya, 1314/1896. Reprint, Cairo: al-Matba'a al-Maymuniyya [Mustafa Baba al-Halabi *et al.*], 1323/1905.

————. *Sahih*. See Ibn Hajar, *Fath al-Bari*.

Al-Busiri. *Misbah al-Zujaja fi Zawa'id Ibn Majah*. 2nd ed. 4 vols. Ed. Muhammad al-Muntaqa al-Kashnawi. Beirut: Dar al-'Arabiyya, 1983.

Al-Daraqutni. *Al-'Ilal*. 9 vols. Ed. Mahfuz al-Rahman Zayn Allah al-Salafi. Riyadh: Dar Tiba, 1985.

————. *Sunan*. 4 vols. in 2. Together with Muhammad Shams al-Haqq al-'Azim Abadi's *al-Ta'liq al-Mughni*. Ed. Al-Sayyid 'Abd Allah Hashim Yamani al-Madani. Beirut: Dar al-Ma'rifa, 1966. Repr. Beirut: Dar Ihya al-Turath al-'Arabi, 1993.

Al-Darimi. *Musnad*. 2 vols. Ed. Fu'ad Ahmad Zamarli and Khalid al-Sab' al-'Ilmi. Beirut: Dar al-Kitab al-'Arabi, 1987.

Al-Dhahabi. *Mizan al-I'tidal*. 4 vols. Ed. 'Ali Muhammad al-Bajawi. Beirut: Dar al-Ma'rifa, 1963.

————. *Siyar A'lam al-Nubala'*. 19 vols. Ed. Muhibb al-Din al-'Amrawi. Beirut: Dar al-Fikr, 1996.

————. *Siyar A'lam al-Nubala'*. 23 vols. Ed. Shu'ayb al-Arna'ut and Muhammad Na'im al-'Araqsusi. Beirut: Mu'assasa al-Risala, 1992-1993.

Al-Ghumari, Ahmad. *Al-Mughir 'ala al-Ahadith al-Mawdu'a fi al-Jami' al-Saghir*. Cairo: Maktaba al-Qahira, 1998. Reprint.

Al-Hakim (al-Naysaburi). *Ma'rifa 'Ulum al-Hadith*, ed. Sayyid Mu'azzam Husayn. Dacca: n.p., 1935.

————. *Al-Mustadrak 'Ala al-Sahihayn*. With al-Dhahabi's *Talkhis al-Mustadrak*. 5 vols. Indexes by Yusuf 'Abd al-Rahman al-Mar'ashli. Beirut: Dar al-Ma'rifa, 1986.

————. *Al-Mustadrak 'Ala al-Sahihayn*. With al-Dhahabi's *Talkhis al-Mustadrak*. 4 vols. Annotations by Mustafa 'Abd al-Qadir 'Ata'. Beirut: Dar al-Kutub al-'Ilmiyya, 1990.

Al-Hakim al-Tirmidhi. *Nawadir al-Usul*. Beirut: Dar Sadir, n.d. Repr. of Istanbul ed.

Al-Haytami, Ahmad. *Al-Fatawa al-Hadithiyya*. Cairo: Mustafa al-Baba al-Halabi, Repr. 1970, 1989.

Al-Haythami, Nur al-Din. *Majma' al-Zawa'id wa Manba' al-Fawa'id*. 3rd ed. 10 vols. Beirut: Dar al-Kitab al-'Arabi, 1982.

Ibn 'Abd al-Barr. *Al-Isti'ab fi Ma'rifa al-Ashab*. 8 vols. in 4. Ed. 'Ali Muhammad al-Bajawi. Beirut: Dar al-Jil, 1992.

Ibn 'Abd al-Salam. *Targhib Ahl al-Islam fi Sukna al-Sham*. Ed. Iyad Khalid al-Tabba'. Beirut and Damascus: Dar al-Fikr, 1992[2].

Ibn Abi 'Asim. *'Ilal al-Hadith*. 2 vols. Ed. Muhibb al-Din al-Khatib. Beirut: Dar al-Ma'rifa, 1985.

Ibn Abi Shayba. *Al-Musannaf*. 7 vols. Ed. Kamal al-Hut. Riyadh: Maktaba al-Rushd, 1989.

Ibn 'Adi. *Al-Kamil fi Du'afa' al-Rijal*. 7 vols. Ed. Yahya Mukhtar Ghazawi. Beirut: Dar al-Fikr, 1988.

Ibn 'Alawi, al-Sayyid Muhammad al-Hasani al-Maliki. See al-Maliki, al-Sayyid Muhammad ibn 'Alawi.

Ibn al-'Arabi, Abu Bakr. *'Arida al-Ahwadhi Sharh Sunan al-Tirmidhi*. 13 vols. Beirut, Dar al-Kutub al-'Ilmiyya, n.d.

Ibn 'Asakir. *Ta'ziya al-Muslim 'an Akhih*. Ed. Majdi Fathi al-Sayyid. Jeddah: Maktaba al-Sahaba, 1991.

Ibn Hajar. *Fath al-Bari Sharh Sahih al-Bukhari*. 14 vols. Notes by 'Abd al-'Aziz ibn Baz. Beirut: Dar al-Kutub al-'Ilmiyya, 1989. Includes al-Bukhari's *Sahih*.

————. *Ibidem*. 13 vols. Ed. Muhammad Fouad 'Abd al-Baqi and Muhibb al-Din al-Khatib. Beirut: Dar al-Ma'rifa, 1959.

————. *Ibidem*. Cairo: al-Matba'a al-Bahiyya, 1348/1929-1930.

————. *Al-Isaba fi Tamyiz al-Sahaba*. 8 vols. Calcutta, 1269/1853.

————. *Lisan al-Mizan*. 7 vols. Hyderabad: Da'ira al-Ma'arif al-Nizamiyya, 1329/1911. Repr. Beirut: Mu'assassa al-A'lami, 1986.

————. *Al-Matalib al-'Aliya*. 4 vols. Kuwait, 1393/1973.

————. *Mukhtasar Zawa'id Musnad al-Bazzar.* 2 vols. Ed. Sabri 'Abd al-Khaliq Abu Dharr. Beirut: Mu'assasa al-Kutub al-Thaqafiyya, 1993.

————. *Tahrir Taqrib al-Tahdhib.* 4 vols. Eds. Bashshar 'Awwad Ma'ruf and Shu'ayb al-Arna'ut. Beirut: Mu'assasa al-Risala, 1997.

————. *Taqrib al-Tahdhib.* Ed. Muhammad 'Awwama. Aleppo: Dar al-Rashid, 1997.

Ibn Hibban. *Sahih Ibn Hibban bi Tartib Ibn Balban.* 18 vols. Ed. Shu'ayb al-Arna'ut. Beirut: Mu'assasa al-Risala, 1993.

Ibn al-Jawzi. *Zad al-Masir fi 'Ilm al-Tafsir.* 3rd ed. 10 vols. Beirut: al-Maktab al-Islami, 1984.

Ibn Kathir. *Tafsir al-Qur'an al-'Azim.* 4 vols. Beirut: Dar al-Fikr, 1981.

Ibn Khuzayma. *Al-Sahih.* 4 vols. Ed. Muhammad Mustafa al-A'zami. Beirut: Al-Maktab al-Islami, 1970.

Ibn Majah. *Sunan.* See al-Suyuti *et al., Sharh Sunan Ibn Majah.*

Ibn al-Mubarak. *Al-Jihad.* Ed. Nazih Hammad. Tunis: Al-Dar al-Tunisiyya, 1972.

————. *Al-Zuhd.* Ed. Habib al-Rahman al-A'zami. Beirut: Dar al-Kutub al-'Ilmiyya, n.d.

Ibn Qayyim al-Jawziyya. *Zad al-Ma'ad fi Hadi Khayr al-'Ibad.* 6 vols. Eds. 'Abd al-Qadir al-Arna'ut and Shu'ayb al-Arna'ut. Beirut: Mu'assasa al-Risala, 1997.

Ibn Qunfudh. *Wasila al-Islam bi al-Nabi 'Alayhi al-Sala wa al-Salam.* Beirut: Dar al-Gharb al-Islami, 1984.

Ibn Sa'd. *Al-Tabaqat al-Kubra.* 8 vols. Beirut: Dar Sadir, n.d.

Isma'il al-Qadi al-Maliki. *Fadl al-Salat 'ala al-Nabi* 🕮. Ed. Muhammad Nasir al-Din al-Albani. Beirut: al-Maktab al-Islami, 1977[3].

Al-Jassas. *Ahkam al-Qur'an.* 5 vols. Ed. Muhammad al-Sadiq Qamhawi. Beirut: Dar Ihya' al-Turath al-'Arabi, 1985. Reprint.

Kabbani, Shaykh Muhammad Hisham. *Encyclopedia of Islamic Doctrine.* 7 vols. Moutain View: Al-Sunna Foundation of America, 1998.

Al-Kattani, al-Sayyid Muhammad ibn Ja'far. *Nazm al-Mutanathir fi al-Hadith al-Mutawatir.* Ed. Sharaf Hijazi. Cairo: Dar al-Kutub al-Salafiyya, n.d. and Beirut: Dar al-Kutub al-'Ilmiyya, 1980.

Al-Khatib al-Baghdadi. *Tarikh Baghdad.* 14 vols. Madina: al-Maktaba al-Salafiyya, n.d. See also al-Ahdab, *Zawa'id Tarikh Baghdad.*

Al-Khattabi. *Ma'alim al-Sunan Sharh Sunan Abi Dawud.* 4 vols. in 2. Ed. 'Abd al-Salam 'Abd al-Shafi Muhammad. Beirut: Dar al-Kutub al-'Ilmiyya, 1996.

Lahmar, Hamid. *Al-Imam Malik Mufassiran.* Beirut: Dar al-Fikr, 1995.

Al-Lalika'i. *Sharh Usul I'tiqad Ahl al-Sunna.* 4 vols. Ed. Ahmad Sa'd Hamdan. Riyadh: Dar Tiba, 1982.

Makhluf, Muhammad Hasanayn. *Fatawa Shar'iyya.* 2 vols. Cairo: Dar al-I'tisam, 1985.

Malik. *Al-Muwatta'.* 2 vols. Ed. Muhammad Fouad 'Abd al-Baqi. Beirut: Dar al-Kutub al-'Ilmiyya, n.d.

Al-Maliki, al-Sayyid Muhammad ibn 'Alawi al-Hasani. *Al-Anwar al-Bahiyya min Isra' wa Mi'raj Khayr al-Bariyya.* Mecca: s.n. 1993.

———. *Mafahim Yajib an Tusahhah.* 4th ed. Dubai: Hashr ibn Muhammad Dalmuk, 1986.

———. *Manhaj al-Salaf fi Fahm al-Nusus Bayn al-Nazariyya wa al-Tatbiq.* N.p.: 1998.

Mamduh, Mahmud Sa'id. *Raf' al-Minara li Takhrij Ahadith al-Tawassul wa al-Ziyara.* 3rd ed. Cairo: Dar al-Imam al-Tirmidhi, 1997.

Al-Maqdisi. *Al-Ahadith al-Mukhtara.* 10 vols. Ed. 'Abd al-Malik ibn Dahish. Mecca: Maktaba al-Nahda al-Haditha, 1990.

Al-Mubarakfuri. *Tuhfa al-Ahwadhi bi Sharh Jami' al-Tirmidhi.* 10 vols. Beirut: Dar al-Kutub al-'Ilmiyya, 1990. Includes al-Tirmidhi's *Sunan.*

Al Munawi. *Fayd al-Qadir.* 2nd ed. 6 vols. Beirut: Dar al Ma'rifa, 1972. Repr. Cairo, 1356/1937 ed.

Al-Mundhiri. *Al-Targhib wa al-Tarhib.* With al-Naji's *Awham al-Targhib.* 5 vols. Ed. Ayman Salih Sha'ban. Cairo: Dar al-Hadith, 1994.

———. *Al-Targhib wa al-Tarhib.* 4 vols. Ed. Ibrahim Shams al-Din. Beirut: Dar al-Kutub al-'Ilmiyya, 1997.

Muslim. *Sahih.* 5 vols. Ed. M. Fuad 'Abd al-Baqi. Beirut: Dar Ihya' al-Turath al-'Arabi, 1954. Also see al-Nawawi, *Sharh Sahih Muslim.*

Al-Nahhas. *Ma'ani al-Qur'an al-Karim.* Ed. Muhammad 'Ali al-Sabuni. Mecca: Jami'a Umm al-Qura, 1989.

Al-Nasa'i. *Sunan.* See al-Suyuti, *Sharh Sunan al-Nasa'i.*

————. *Al-Sunan al-Kubra*. 6 vols. Eds. 'Abd al-Ghaffar Sulayman al-Bandari and Sayyid Kisrawi Hasan. Beirut: Dar al-Kutub al-'Ilmiyya, 1991.

Al-Nawawi. *Sharh Sahih Muslim*. 18 vols. Ed. Khalil al-Mays. Beirut: Dar al-Kutub al-'Ilmiyya, n.d. Includes Muslim's *Sahih*.

————. *Sharh Sahih Muslim*. 18 vols. Beirut: Dar Ihya' al-Turath al-'Arabi, 1972.

————. *Tahdhib al-Asma' wa al-Lughat*. Cairo: Idara al-Tiba'a al-Muniriyya, [1927?].

Nu'aym ibn Hammad al-Marwazi. *Kitab al-Fitan*. 2 vols. Ed. Samir Amin al-Zuhri. Cairo: Maktaba al-Tawhid, 1992.

Al-Qari. *Jam' al-Wasa'il fi Sharh al-Shama'il*. A commentary on Tirmidhi's *al-Shama'il*. Cairo, 1317/1899.

————. *Mirqat al-Mafatih Sharh Mishkat al-Masabih*. 5 vols. Ed. Muhammad al-Zuhri al-Ghamrawi. Cairo: al-Matba'a al-Maymuniyya, 1309/1892. Reprint Beirut: Dar Ihya' al-Turath al-'Arabi, n.d.

————. *Mirqat al-Mafatih Sharh Mishkat al-Masabih*. Together with Ibn Hajar's *Ajwiba 'Ala Risala al-Qazwini Hawla Ba'd Ahadith al-Masabih*. 11 vols. Ed. Sidqi Muhammad Jamil al-'Attar. Damascus: Dar al-Fikr, 1994.

Al-Qurtubi. *Al-Jami' li Ahkam al-Qur'an*. 2nd ed. 20 vols. Ed. Ahmad 'Abd al-'Alim al-Barduni. Cairo: Dar al-Sha'b and Beirut: Dar Ihya' al-Turath al-'Arabi, 1952-1953. Reprint.

Al-Raba'i. *Fada'il al-Sham wa Dimashq*. Ed. M. Nasir al-Din al-Albani. Beirut: al-Maktab al-Islami, 1985[4].

Al-Ramahurmuzi. *Al-Muhaddith al-Fasil*. Ed. Muhammad al-Khatib. Beirut: Dar al-Fikr, 1984[3].

Al-Sakhawi, Muhammad ibn 'Abd al-Rahman. *Al-Maqasid al-Hasana*. Ed. Muhammad 'Uthman al-Khisht. Beirut: Dar al-Kitab al-'Arabi, 1985.

————. *Al-Qawl al-Badi' fi al-Salat 'ala al-Habib al-Shafi'*. Beirut: Dar al-Kutub al-'Ilmiyya, 1987.

Al-Shawkani. *Fath al-Qadir al-Jami' Bayna Fannay al-Riwaya wa al-Diraya min 'Ilm al-Tafsir*. 5 vols. Beirut: Dar al-Fikr, n.d.

————. *Nayl al-Awtar*.

Siraj al-Din, 'Abd Allah. *al-Salat 'ala al-Nabi* 🕌. Aleppo: Dar al-Falah, 1995[2].

Al-Suyuti, Jalal al-Din. *Asrar Tartib al-Qur'an.* Ed. 'Abd al-Qadir Ahmad 'Ata. Cairo: Dar al-I'tisam, n.d.

————. *Al-Dibaj 'ala Sahih Muslim ibn al-Hajjaj.* 6 vols. Ed. Abu Ishaq al-Juwayni al-Athari. Al-Khubar: Dar Ibn 'Affan, 1996.

————. *Al-Durr al-Manthur fi al-Tafsir al-Ma'thur.* 8 vols. Beirut: Dar al-Fikr, 1994.

————. *Al-Khabar al-Dall 'ala Wujud al-Qutb wa al-Awtad wa al-Nujaba' wa al-Abdal.* Ed. 'Abd Allah Muhammad al-Siddiq al-Ghumari al-Hasani. Cairo: Maktaba al-Qahira, 1997.

————. *Al-La'ali' al-Masnu'a fi al-Ahadith al-Mawdu'a.* 2 vols. Beirut: Dar al-Ma'rifa, 1983.

————. *Manahil al-Safa fi Takhrij Ahadith al-Shifa.* Beirut, 1988.

————. *Mufhimat al-Aqran fi Mubhamat al-Qur'an.* Ed. Iyad Khalid al-Tabba'. Beirut: Mu'assasa al-Risala, 1991.

————. *Sharh Sunan al-Nasa'i.* 9 vols. Ed. 'Abd al-Fattah Abu Ghudda. Aleppo & Beirut: Maktab al-Matbu'at al-Islamiyya, 1986. Includes al-Nasa'is' *Sunan.*

————. *Al-Ta'aqqubat 'ala al-Mawdu'at.* Ed. Sayyid Muhammad Maqshawqa'li. India: al-Matba' al-'Alawi, 1303/1886.

————. *Tafsir al-Jalalayn.* Cairo: Dar al-Hadith, n.d.

————, 'Abd al-Ghani al-Dihlawi, and Fakhr al-Hasan al-Gangohi. *Sharh Sunan Ibn Majah.* Karachi: Qadimi Kutub Khana, n.d. Includes Ibn Majah's *Sunan.*

Al-Tabarani. *Al-Mu'jam al-Awsat.* 10 vols. Eds. Tariq ibn 'Awad Allah and 'Abd al-Muhsin ibn Ibrahim al-Husayni. Cairo: Dar al-Haramayn, 1995.

————. *Al-Mu'jam al-Kabir.* 20 vols. Ed. Hamdi ibn 'Abd al-Majid al-Salafi. Mosul: Maktaba al-'Ulum wa al-Hikam, 1983.

————. *Al-Mu'jam al-Saghir.* 2 vols. Ed. Muhammad Shakur Mahmud. Beirut and Amman: Al-Maktab al-Islami, Dar 'Ammar, 1985.

————. *Musnad al-Shamiyyin.* 2 vols. Ed. Hamdi ibn 'Abd al-Majid al-Salafi. Beirut: Mu'assasa al-Risala, 1984.

Al-Tabari, Muhammad ibn Jarir. *Jami' al-Bayan fi Tafsir al-Qur'an.* 30 vols. Beirut: Dar al-Ma'arif, 1980; Dar al-Fikr, 1985.

Al-Tabari, Muhibb al-Din. *Al-Riyad al-Nadira.* 2 vols. Ed. 'Isa al-Humayri. Beirut: Dar al-Gharb al-Islami, 1996.

Al-Tahawi. *Mushkil al-Athar*. Hyderabad: Da'ira al-Ma'arif al-'Uthmaniyya, 1915.

Al-Tayalisi. *Musnad*. Beirut: Dar al-Kitab al-Lubnani; Dar al-Ma'rifa; Dar al-Tawfiq, n.d. All three are reprints of the 1321/1903 edition of Da'ira al-Ma'arif al-'Uthmaniyya in Hyderabad.

Tayyim, As'ad Salim. *Bayan Awham al-Albani fi Tahqiqihi li Kitab Fadl al-Salat 'ala al-Nabi li al-Qadi Isma'il ibn Ishaq al-Azdi. Wa Yalihi Takhrij Hadith Aws al-Thaqafi fi Fadl al-Jumu'a*. Amman: Dar al-Razi, 1999.

Al-Tha'alibi. *Jawahir al-Hisan fi Tafsir al-Qur'an*. Beirut: Mu'assasa al-A'lami, n.d.

Al-Thawri. *Tafsir*. Ed. Imtiyaz 'Ali 'Arshi. Ramapur: Maktaba al-Rida, n.d. Repr. Beirut: Dar al-Kutub al-'Ilmiyya, 1983.

Al-Tirmidhi. *Al-Shama'il al-Muhammadiyya wa al-Khasa'il al-Mustafawiyya*. Ed. Sayyid 'Abbas al-Jalimi. Beirut: Mu'assasa al-Kutub al-Thaqafiyya, 1992.

———. *Al-Sunan*. See al-Mubarakfuri, *Tuhfa al-Ahwadhi*.

Al-'Uqayli, *al-Du'afa' min al-Ruwat*. 4 vols. Ed. 'Abd al-Mu'it Amin Qal'aji. Beirut: Dar al-Kutub al-'Ilmiyya, 1984.

Al-Wahidi. *Asbab al-Nuzul*. Ed. Ayman Salih Sha'ban. Cairo: Dar al-Hadith, 1996.

———. *Al-Wajiz fi Tafsir al-Kitab al-'Aziz*. 2 vols. Ed. Safwan 'Adnan Dawudi. Damascus and Beirut: Dar al-Qalam and al-Dar al-Shamiyya, 1995.

Yaqut al-Hamawi. *Mu'jam al-Buldan*. 5 vols. Beirut: Dar al-Fikr, n.d.

Printed in the United States
124637LV00009B/126/A